# The Rustling of Leaves

# The Rustling of Leaves

## An Adventure of Recovery

*Frank Costanzo*

Writer's Showcase presented by *Writer's Digest*
San Jose  New York  Lincoln  Shanghai

# The Rustling of Leaves
### An Adventure of Recovery

Published by Writer's Showcase presented by *Writer's Digest*
an imprint of iUniverse.com, Inc.

For information address:
iUniverse.com, Inc.
620 North 48th Street
Suite 201
Lincoln, NE 68504-3467
www.iuniverse.com

ISBN: 0-595-09984-X

Printed in the United States of America

*One day old Skeeter said to me, "Always be aware of the rustling of the leaves and find shelter from the coming storm." All my life I remembered what he told me; yet it seemed that when, all the world was bright and sunny around me a slight wind would be rustling the leaves under my feet, I would forget Skeeter's advice and soon find myself naked, trying to survive a raging storm.*

# *Prologue*

*Northern California, Monday morning, March 1, 1971*: I opened my eyes, barely. My mouth felt parched from the cheap gin. It seemed that my whole body was dehydrated. I wasn't sure where I was. Every bone in my body ached. When I figured out that I was lying in my ugly little rented room, I realized I must have had another grand mal seizure after finishing the bottle.

I tried prayer:"Please, God, I'm having two seizures a day, what am I going to do? I'm probably going to die. So what? Why don't you just let me die, anything is better than this."

I knew the seizures were a direct result of the drinking, but I just couldn't-or wouldn't-stop. The reason I drank made very little difference anymore. I tried to get up, but was too weak. I couldn't remember the last time I had eaten. I finally pulled myself together enough to drag what was left of my body onto the chair. I was in my shorts. As I looked down at myself I could see that my ribs were sticking through my skin. My six-foot one-inch frame couldn't have weighed more than 140 pounds. I was shaking violently.

I struggled to the sink and drank as much water as I could without vomiting, holding the glass with both hands. I lost control and watched it without caring while it broke in the sink. My mind had suddenly begun to scream at me to find a drink. Had my roommate left me anything? If I just could have a couple of pulls from a bottle I could muster enough strength to go around the corner and get a fifth. I flopped back down in the chair to avoid falling or passing out.

I was starting to become panicky. I thought I need to look for the bottle, but I can't get out of the chair. Please, God, even one drink would be enough. I promise to be satisfied with only one. Oh, God, I'm sure I can pull myself together with even one. I know there has to be a bottle around here somewhere. All I need to do is get up and look. I'm just so sick I can't move. What am I going to do? God, stop being an asshole! Show me where that bottle is, or I'll die." I was obviously hallucinating. I saw my seven-year-old son, Frank John, in the room. I shouted, Frank John, Thank God your here. Help me find the bottle. I hurled myself from the chair to grab him. I ran full force into the wall and knocked myself out.

I looked around the room. All I could see was the ceiling. I was lying flat on my back. I was still shaking, but I was calmer than I had been before: I didn't know whether having another drink was such a good idea. I hadn't toyed with a thought as radical as that for as long as I could remember. I was bare ass naked in the middle of a raging storm I had created, and the time had come for me to make up my mind to simply die or to ask for help somewhere. There seemed to be nothing to live for. Ginger had left with the kids, the house had been foreclosed, the business was bankrupt, the servants had left, the cars had been repossessed, business associates wanted nothing to do with me, I couldn't even imagine the amount of debts I owed. I had lost all my self-respect. I didn't deserve to live. Do I really deserve to live?" I asked myself, "I don't know, but I think something's telling me that I should take a run at it, anyway."

I don't remember much of what happened in the next hour or so. Somehow I dressed and went to the corner phone booth, but can't recall doing so. My next recollection was sitting inside-as I didn't have the strength to stand-talking for the next two hours to a woman in some twelve step program. I don't know how I even knew this program existed. I don't know how I found the phone number and dialed it, but I did.

That evening a man and his wife came to the room to talk. I had eaten nothing, I was shaking violently. They took me to a restaurant and I ate a hamburger. I threw it up promptly after leaving. The man and wife spoke to me in very quiet tones, and even though I felt I was close to death, they assured me I was not going to die. They added that probably over the next few days there would be times when I wished I would die. They were right on both counts: since that day I never found it necessary to drink alcohol again. They took me to a twelve step meeting but I have no recollection of what took place.

The man and the woman returned the next evening and brought me a another twelve step meeting. I had one seizure that day, still continued to hallucinate, but somehow had refrained from drinking alcohol. Even though I was sick from the effects of alcohol abuse, and my body ached from the seizures, I felt better than the previous day. At least I was beginning to walk without assistance. I began to have hope that I would actually recover. I knew in my heart that had I not made the phone call, and asked for help; I probably would have been dead. After the twelve step meeting that evening, people crowded around me: offering words of encouragement. I was given a cup of coffee but was shaking so bad that I couldn't hold the cup. Someone kept putting spoonfulls of honey in my mouth. After the meeting four or five men took me to a coffee shop close by; talking constantly about what I should do to avoid drinking alcohol over the next 24 hours. Before we left they had decided that I needed a sponsor-whatever that meant-right away, so they appointed the man sitting next to me to serve temporarily. I just nodded my head affirmatively, as I had no idea what they were talking about. He was about my age, nice appearance, and it was easy to see that he worked in the construction industry.(actually, he was an excellent carpenter, turned handyman, to allow himself more time to work with other recovering alcoholics) He was quiet and unassuming, but you could see passion in his eyes when he spoke.

As we drove home he spoke a great deal about how to stay sober during the first few days, then in a very casual manner, glanced at me, and inquired if while sitting in the meeting, had I seen anyone that might need my help. I must admit that I was startled at his comment, and answered, "I'm sorry, I felt so sick, and was shaking so badly that I had trouble seeing across the table. It took every bit of effort for me to even hold a coffee cup. If anyone in that room needed help tonight, it certainly had to be me."

"Oh, but your wrong," he replied, "your problems were obvious, so you were receiving a great deal of attention. If you had been observant, and not so consumed with yourself, you would have realized that there were two or three people there that had only a week or so of sobriety, and, although they did not have the physical problems you have, required as much attention as you. I had no idea where this conversation was leading, but kept quiet, and he continued, "Tomorrow I want you to start looking around that room for people in that condition. After the meeting, no matter how bad you personally feel: go to them, put a smile on your face, ask them how they're doing, and listen with compassion when they tell you their problems." I was totally confused. Why would he want me to do such a silly thing? With all the real sober people around, why would anyone who was new want to talk to me? I would have just a couple of sober days by then, be physically sick, be shaking like a leaf, and scared to death. The idea sounded ridiculous, but I kept quiet about my reservations. I tried to smile, and said, "Okay, if that's what you want, I'll do it." I left the matter at that. He picked me up the next evening to go to another twelve step meeting. I had another seizure that day, but the shaking had subsided somewhat. I was eating again, sleeping most of the day, and had gone to the doctor for a vitamin shot-at my new sponsor's suggestion-so I wasn't feeling quite so sick. While driving to the meeting, he mentioned nothing about the previous evening's conversation, but I still was determined to do what he told me the night before. He had such a great smile, and seemed so caring; coupled with the fact that I had no illusions how I had been snatched from certain death a few days before. I figured I had better not press my luck.

In the meeting I tried to concentrate on what was being said, while looking for someone in as bad a shape as I. I was having a difficult time on both counts. My powers of concentration were almost nonexistent, coupled with the fact that I was sure no one could feel as awful as my poor body felt. All at once my eyes focused on a young man, about my age, his eyes staring vacantly around the room while twirling a pack of cigarettes in front of him, around and around and around. He looked gaunt and sick. I knew from long experience what he was thinking. He was wondering how fast he could get out of there so he could find something to drink. The look was unmistakable. The twelve step meeting lasted another 20 minutes. I continued staring at him. He didn't see me or anyone else; his mind was too filled with the bottle he planned to drink somewhere outside of the room where he was now sitting. I knew that each minute was a hour to him because I had been in that place more times than I wanted to remember.

The meeting ended and I was out of my seat as fast as my not to stable body would transport me, determined to talk with him before he left the room. I walked up to him, feebly groped his arm, and said, "Hi, I'm Frank. I'm brand new to all of this. Could you help me?"

He mumbled something under his breath, while trying to push my hand away, and replied anxiously, "I'm new, too. Why don't you try to talk with someone who knows more about what's going on? I'm in kind of a hurry."

"Please," I persisted, "It wont take long. I really need to talk with someone who is new like me." I continued to retain my hold on his arm.

"Okay," he relented reluctantly, "what do you need."

Under the circumstances I wasn't exactly sure what to say, so I said the first thing that came to my mind, "Well, I wanted to know how long you've been sober."

Somewhat irritated, he said, "This is my tenth day."

"Wow!" I wasn't putting him on because 10 days sober sounded like a lifetime to me right then. "How did you get through the first few days?"

He looked at me in a strange manner, then began to smile for the first time all evening. He spent the next 10 minutes relating his struggles over the last few days. When he had finished I asked him if he had a sponsor yet, and he answered, "No." "Boy, I've got a great one." I said, even though I had no idea what a sponser did. "We're going to coffee together right now. Why don't you come with us. Maybe he'll be your sponsor, too." He hesitated for a moment, thinking of the bottle that was waiting for him, then relaxed, broke out in a big grin, and said, "Sure, why not? That sounds okay." The three of us went to a coffee shop and talked until midnight. He asked my sponsor to become his sponsor, too, and an agreement was struck.

When I arrived home that evening I was ecstatic, floating on a pink cloud. The aching in my body remained, but I no longer felt sick. I had helped someone! It was the greatest high that I have ever experienced. My new friend would have gone back to drinking if I hadn't recognized what he was about to do, and talked to him. Once again, I felt that the world had a use for me.

I met my sponsor at his house the next day and he told me he wanted me to begin working the Twelve Steps. I hadn't the slightest idea as to what he was talking about and told him so. He proceeded to quote the First Step, "We admitted we were powerless over alcohol-and our lives had become unmanageable."

He advised me that each morning-upon awakening-I should find a quiet place; somewhere very personal. He told me to spend 5 minutes, eyes closed, remaining completely still; attempting to meditate. He told me to clear my mind of all thoughts. He chuckled when he said that in the beginning I would be lucky to achieve 5 seconds, much less 5 minutes, of clearing my mind completely. Nevertheless, I was to continue the process each day. He was right. I couldn't believe how long 5 minutes would become, just sitting with my eyes closed, trying to think of nothing.

He had bought me some pencils and a pad of paper. He told me to keep them close by. When the meditation period ended I should write down the first thought that came to my mind of any incident during my addiction; a time when I had become totally powerless to stop drinking.

That certainly didn't seem to be much problem; the reason I was sitting there was that I was unable to quit using alcohol. He told me not to reread what I wrote or I would probably change what I had written; adding or deleting to better suit my conscience recollection. I did exactly what he told me to do every morning for about two weeks. On the fourteenth day I spent 5 minutes meditating as best I could, picked up the pad of paper and began to read what I had written. I was shocked! I couldn't believe what was on the paper. "Was this person I'm reading about really me? It couldn't be! I know I had a bad drinking problem but, my God, could I have been so totally helpless in coping with my situation." What follows is a few of the items I wrote: I was once told by my doctor that I would die in less than a year if I didn't stop drinking. After leaving his office I went to a bar and got drunk while I contemplated what he had told me; some of my employees once found me lying in a pile of old bricks. I had no idea how I got there, but must have been there for a day or so. They brought me into the construction shack where I had a seizure after insisting on just one more drink. They took me to the hospital. When I woke up I demanded to be released. I immediately went out and got drunk, again. I have no recollection of what happened in the few days that followed.

For the first time I realized the truth about myself; the truth which I believe was told to me by my Spiritual, not intellectual, Conscious. There was no question that I was an alcoholic, powerless over it's use. The problem far exceeded my admission of just having trouble quitting. For the first time I understood that my body craved it, and would push me to insanity or death to get it. I became grateful to comprehend this truth at last, and I admitted the truth to my innermost self. I had taken the first half of the First Step, and secured for myself a solid foundation for moving forward.

When I realized that as part of the First Step it would also be necessary to admit that my life had become unmanageable, I felt uncomfortable and preferred to ignore the whole issue. After all, hadn't I already admitted I was powerless? It seemed that I was being put through a great deal of unnecessary humiliation. Wasn't enough, enough? Just because my life had deteriorated to the level of a street person facing death and insanity shouldn't imply that when I use alcohol my life was unmanageable. Somewhat unruly I admit, but definitely not unmanageable.

My sponsor explained that unmanageability, as it is used in the context of the First Step, has very little to do with paying bills on time, having adequate housing accommodations or being employed. A manageable life goes back to the fundamental human concept of the Golden Rule, compassion and caring for others. Yet, unless I'm free from my addictions and obsessions, I will always take care of my own needs before thinking of anyone else's. I tried to convince him that the problems in my life were not the result of unmanageability, but were probably caused by my unruly behavior. He told me that he appreciated my well thought out theory as to my character when I drank, but suggested that the theory had a minor flaw or two. He told me to spend the next two weeks meditating each morning for 5 minutes, keeping the pad and pencil close by. He recommended that after each meditation I should write the first incident that came to my mind as to how I treated some other human being when I was drinking. He cautioned me to try and eliminate right, wrong, good, bad, guilt or emotion from the writing. "Try to remember that what you are writing is what was, not what is. You are searching for the truth of your former life." Judging from my experience, I was now finding out just how powerless I was over alcohol through my writings on the first half of the First Step. Last week, I had an uncomfortable feeling as I left his house that I would begin to see that my relationship with others would be different than what I had always envisioned them to be. I was right.

I found those writings to be very painful as they revealed the truth about my treatment of family and friends. Later on in the week, after 5 minutes of meditation, with tears flowing down my cheeks, I read what I had written. I'll share one of the writings: I was losing our family home in foreclosure without telling my wife Ginger. It was a magnificent house, and was her pride and joy. I owed very little, and the mortgage holder was a friend. He begged me to come in to his office to work out some arrangement. Instead, being almost totally paranoid from the alcohol, I left town, got a hotel room, and spent the week drinking alone in the room while the house was foreclosed. After reading that story and several others just as terrible, I immediately admitted that when I drank alcohol my life became totally unmanageable.

*Folsom Prison, Fourteen Years Later:* Most of the words that explain the feelings of going to prison have already been overused, and I can't use them now because they don't describe how I feel. It is easy to explain how I felt when I was first arrested almost three years ago. I was obsessed-obsessed with the need to fight and the lust for revenge. Those addictions were removed a few months into the almost two years spent in endless hearings and a long trial: I have reestablished the Twelve Step disciplines in my life that gave me the ability to face the ordeal, and I became more and more serene to the madness around me.

Because I practiced those disciplines, today I have as full a life as anyone can have in a maximum security prison. I receive, and respond to, a minimum of ten letters each day, many from friends and relatives with whom I had lost contact many years ago. Despite all the time I would seem to have being locked down in this cell each day, I can't imagine where I will find the time to thank all the people who sent me Christmas cards. It's amazing! I have taped them to the wall of the cell in the form of a Christmas tree. My cellmate will not say it, but I know he enjoys the Christmas spirit those cards provide. He's been sitting in this prison a long time.

At first blush I thought that writing a book in Folsom Prison was an excellent idea, especially a book that is intended to carry a message. I must admit, however, that the atmosphere here is about as conducive to sharing a message as I am qualified to write about one. Most men at fifty years old are thinking of retirement, gardening, and travel. Messages by men of that age who sit in a cell in Folsom Prison are highly suspect. Each day here at Folsom there are stickings-that's the word used for stabbings-sometimes ending in death, and there are the inevitable rapes. There are violent gangs. There are guard towers every couple hundred feet with M-14s sticking out of the windows, pointed at the general population, held by angry men in uniforms who are prepared to and do use them. There are catwalks everywhere with the same type of gentlemen, wearing the same type of uniform, holding the same type of weapon, prepared to do the same type of thing that the gentle-men in the towers are prepared to do.

Johnny Cash's song about living in Folsom Prison did not underes-timate this joint. When I first came here I thought it was awesome. That's not exactly true; actually, I arrived in the middle of the night, in the middle of the winter, so I didn't see much. They brought us in on a bus, took off our chains, then took our clothes. We stood outside the receiving department while they issued red jumpsuits and bedding to the inmates, two at a time, while the rest of us stood out in the cold, stark naked. My teeth were chattering, and I didn't care a whole lot about how awesome Folsom was; my only thought was to find some place in these ugly granite walls with a little heat. Then some uniformed clown stood in front of us, warning us to toughen up because we were now in Folsom. I thought about flipping him off, but my fingers were too numb.

The next morning, while we were being led to the chow hall from our elite accommodations on Fish Row (where new inmates live) high up on the fifth tier, I had thawed out, so I had a better look at the granite walls and the catwalks with the somber-looking men holding their weapons. I was fascinated by the inmates in the cells. Maybe James Cagney or Humphrey Bogart would walk around the corner any minute and say, "You'll never take me alive, coppa!"

Folsom Prison has several avantages to offer an aspiring author. I have a great deal of time on my hands. I leave my cell for work at 8:00 a.m. and return at 2:30 p.m. Except for breakfast and dinner, which take about a half-hour each, my remaining time is spent in my cell. My accommodations are quite nice, I am told, as prisons go. I live in one of the original cells built when the prison was constructed in 1860. It is a bit larger than the newer cells in which I was first housed, in one of the other cell blocks. The major difference is that this cell is constructed with huge granite blocks, no windows, and a steel door with a couple of slits to slide mail through and three air holes. Living here is like living in a tomb. If I was claustrophobic I'm sure I'd have gone stark, raving mad by this time. Maybe I have. There are people who accuse me of madness in or out of this cell, anyway.

My cellmate is a nice guy who has been here or in other institutions most of his life. We work together in the administration office and are pretty good friends. He is a college graduate, clean and courteous, and when we converse, which is not often, he usually has something interesting to say. We are not "roaddogs"(best friends), though. No one in this whole joint would have me as a roaddog on a bet, because I'm only a first-termer in a maximum security prison. With few exceptions, most inmates here have grown up in the prison system and know all the unwritten rules that anyone living this life should know through years of exposure. I've been in prison for only the last two months and am completely uneducated in being a professional convict-for instance, I smile a lot. I even walk into the chow hall with a smile on my face; I usually get nothing but frowns in return. No one smiles in here. There is a great deal of laughter from dirty jokes, but almost no genuine smiles, no genuine laughter. My smiling is going to be one character defect that is difficult to correct-not that I intend to correct it. I enjoy it. The other day I almost got shot. It was raining, and I started running through the yard to my job to avoid getting soaked. It's not as if they give courses on what and what not to do. How was I to know that running is forbidden? There certainly aren't any signs. The guards in the gun towers assume someone running has just stuck someone else and is running away from the scene. Their orders are to shoot, which I guess makes sense to them, but if they would have had the courtesy to inquire, I'd have explained that all I was doing was trying to get out of the rain. I heard the gunfire and knew the gun towers were shooting. I hit the ground, finding myself lying face down in the mud. Most of the men I work with were watching from the window of the assignment office. They thought my near brush with death was hilarious. They decided to nickname me "Maddog," probably because of my aggressive behavior and prison savvy. They kid me a lot, but I don't mind because even though I'm green as grass, I'm not afraid of living here or of anyone else who is living here, for that matter, and I don't snivel about how tough life is, as do most first-termers. I am readily accepted and have good rapport or at least a good working relationship with almost everyone. On the other hand, who wants a road dog who doesn't know even the basic fundamentals and gets shot at? I can understand how they feel. I know it won't take me long to figure how to live here-if not comfortably, then with my usual flair for being alive.

After the little incident in the rain, my cellmate was pretty disgusted with my lack of education and has begun schooling me on certain matters that even common schoolchildren should know, such as how to react to the aggressor if you are stuck. Since getting stuck is a definite possibility here, I have decided to listen to these simple instructions. If you are stuck, keep moving forward; it's harder for the aggressor to pull out the shank and keep sticking you if you are moving toward him than if you are running away. My cellmate also instructed me how to twist my hand if I happen to hit someone in the face. You know-simple things like that. It's embarrassing, not being a hardened criminal and all that. But who's perfect?

I've read many books and seen many movies about prison violence, and of course violence abounds here. I'm sure that what I write would be much more sensational if I described the terrible people I meet and the incredible abuse they deal out, but that would not be honest. I have not seen the media version of what I see within these walls. Most inmates I meet-whether white, black, or Chicano-are just trying to do their time and return home. Most try to mind their own business, with the full realization that they should always be wary. I would be foolish not to say that a curtain of fear pervades this place and always hangs heavy in everyone's mind. But that fear is created by a small percentage of the inmates, usually gang members prodded by "shot callers," the supposed honchos who decide who gets hit. There are also certain guards who delight in creating more tension than is necessary, but they too are a minority.

My first encounter with violence occurred on the day I was transferred from Fish Row. The guy I celled with as a fish and I had been issued blues, as opposed to the red jumpsuits of the fish, and assigned cells. We agreed to meet later out in the yard to go exploring. I was anxious to start, so I dumped my bedding in the cell and cautiously walked toward the yard. I was amazed! The yard looked about the size of a postage stamp and seemed to be wall-to-wall people, except in the middle.

In the middle of the yard was a dinky grass baseball field and a track that could not have measured 200 yards in circumference. No one was allowed on the grass, and most of the inmates didn't care to use their time running or walking around the track, so everyone was crowded around the periphery. The crowd was so bad it reminded me of the crowds leaving a Forty-Niners' game-only this crowd wasn't leaving.

I am told that the prison had been originally built to house less than 400, and the population now was over 3,000. For the 3,000 prisoners there are approximately 1,500 jobs, leaving half the prison population with nothing to do but mill around in the yard during the day while the other half works. Some men are not assigned jobs for many years, if ever. On weekends, the workers use the yard during the day, and the unemployed are locked down in their cells from Friday evening until Monday morning.

I was surprised at the number of gun towers, although I gave the guns protruding from them only a glance. Right from the first day, inside the building as a fish, I became accustomed to seeing uniformed men with guns in their hands on the catwalks all around me, even in the chow hall as I ate.

The next thing to impress me was the imposing presence of the SHU (Security Housing Unit), a huge granite building that looks like a medieval dungeon. That is the end of the world in the California state prison system. If you are a so-called incorrigible in any other joint, you eventually are sent to the SHU. In Folsom, if you are caught sticking someone, instead of being charged with a crime in a legitimate court, you are just sent to the SHU for a year or so-the theory being that with the enormous number of stickings each week here, it would be impractical to file criminal charges against everyone unless a death occurs. From what I understand, the conditions aren't too bad in there, not as bad as "the hole" we all have read about at one time or another, but I've decided I'd prefer not to partake of that hospitality.

My fish friend came out to the yard shortly after I did, and I could tell he was frightened. He was a heroin addict from San Francisco whose criminal career consisted of petty robberies and burglaries committed to feed his habit. Physically, he was gaunt; his last run with the needle left him about eighty pounds underweight and completely paranoid. His crimes were relatively minor and he did not belong in Folsom. He was told that he would probably be transferred to a minimum security joint in a very few days when a bed opened there. He had a great sense of humor, and now that he was through withdrawal he was excellent company when his paranoia didn't kick in to make him certain that everyone on the yard was about to stick him. I told him to try to settle down so we could go exploring, or just go back to his cell until he was transferred out.

We ran into someone we had met on Fish Row who had been transferred onto the yard a couple days earlier. He was a wily old convict, even though he could not have been older than thirty-five. He was a drug addict, like my friend, but was accustomed to living in the atmosphere of maximum security prisons. We walked through a crowded area where four Chicanos were somehow playing handball in, out, and around the milling crowd. We turned in front of the SHU. I peeked through the front door and was unable to see anything. I thought it would be interesting to see brutal guards beating helpless prisoners with rubber hoses, but no luck. We continued onward, squirming through the mass of humanity, past a basketball game on one side and three sets of bleachers on the other. Each set of bleachers was filled with inmates and completely segregated: one for white, one for black, one for Chicano. I remember wondering what would happen if I just went over and sat in the bleachers other than white. I never acted on the impulse.

As we came to the corner of the SHU we saw an alley-called Blood Alley-formed by one side of the SHU and the facing side of the prison laundry. The alley was about 50 feet wide and ran down to the weight pile, where a large number of inmates spend their yard-time pumping iron. Card and domino players sat at the small tables that lined the alley. Blood Alley is difficult to cover from the gun towers. It's the best place to stick someone.

I glanced over to the side of the SHU, where a metal basket similar to the ones used in ski resorts to take injured skiers off the slopes was hanging on the side of the building. These baskets are hanging everywhere in the prison and are used as stretchers after stickings, to carry the victim to the hospital and, by doing so, I would imagine, to return the area to normal before a riot has a chance to start. For me they serve as a reminder that stickings happen almost daily here, and I should always be aware of the dangers taking place around me.

My friend didn't have the stomach to try exploring Blood Alley, so we decided to break out of the crowds and take a walk around the track. Halfway around the first lap I heard some strange noises-"pop-pop-pop." Immediately the yard became strangely quiet and everyone around me was kneeling down. I was curious as to what was taking place, and had begun to walk toward some commotion across the grass field near the alley when my wily convict friend, who was kneeling down, grabbed my arm and pulled me, yelling, "God damn it, get down or they'll shoot you! There's been a sticking."

I slipped on the grass and fell face down into the mud. When I looked up, two uniformed men were running past me toward the alley. I heard a few more popping sounds. It suddenly occurred to me that the popping was the sound of gunfire from the towers; the guards were attempting to disperse the crowd. I wasn't afraid, but I felt like a complete jerk; why hadn't I recognized the sound of gunfire without having to be told? By the time I was up on one knee, like everyone else, rubbing the mud off my face, I looked over to see a metal stretcher being carried toward the entrance of the prison proper. It contained a young Chicano kid who was obviously in worse shock than I was.

Suddenly everyone got up from the kneeling position and resumed exactly what they had been doing before, as if nothing had occurred. The group on the track in front of us took up their same pace, the man holding the basketball threw it to the man he had originally intended to throw it to, and when I looked over, the handball game was proceeding unhindered. After wiping the mud off my nose, I turned around to find that my dope addict friend had thrown up and was shaking uncontrollably. All he could think of was to get back to the safety of his cell. It made me feel better about myself for being so dumb. At least I hadn't been afraid and wasn't sniveling. He returned to his cell and didn't come out until he was transferred three days later.

My cellmate usually spends most of his time watching television. I have no television set and have little interest in one. His television set sits at the end of his bunk below me. He is quite considerate and always wears earphones so the cell remains quiet. He would let me watch if I cared to, but I'm always too busy with correspondence and reading. I have the top bunk, having less seniority. The mirror over the sink reflects the images from the set below so I don't even have to get off my bunk to watch, except the letters in the commercials are always backward. Early in our infrequent conversations I suggested two interior decorating changes. At the time my cellmate could not believe I was serious because the suggestions were pretty radical. My first suggestion was that we have someone in the arts and crafts department paint two landscapes, with frames, to mount at the end of each of our bunks. That way, instead of staring at the granite blocks, we would enjoy the illusion that we are looking through a window into a meadow on a winter's day. As time went on we could have scenes of other seasons painted to slip in and out of the frames when we tired of the present ones.

My second suggestion was more tricky. It is winter, and because of the granite construction, this cell stays reasonably warm. Nevertheless, we usually make a cup of hot chocolate before turning in for the evening. The prison canteen carries instant cocoa that can be mixed with hot water-not quite what mother use to make, but a more than reasonable treat, considering the circumstances. My thought was to engage the arts and crafts department once again to construct a small potbellied stove of cardboard. We could bring it in past the guards piece by piece, then put it together inside the cell. We could line the bottom of the inside of the stove with cigarette tinfoil, then have someone in the electric shop steal us an extension cord and a red light bulb to hang above the foil. I haven't figured out how to make the light spin, but of course I have time to work out the details. In here, there's always plenty of time.

Once this stove is completed, it would allow us, before we have our evening cocoa, to turn off the light in the cell, turn on the light in the stove, and imagine that we are sitting around a fire chatting while we look out our window and watch the snow fall in the meadow. Sooner or later everything would be discovered and confiscated, but what the hell? We could have it all reconstructed, bring it in again, and enjoy it until it is confiscated again.

As I reflect upon my present circumstances, I guess Folsom Prison does offer an atmosphere conducive to sharing a message, after all. The message is a simple one: with the proper perspective, anyone can enjoy his life, *no matter what the adversity.*

An old retired Coast Guard chief told me this: "You can't kick a dead dog. When he's alive he'll growl and snap and bite. You'll kick him and maybe he'll go away because it's usually nothing but a game. But when the dog dies, the game is over." What happened to me was also just a game: the game of Cops and Robbers. I learned that this game was as ill-conceived as the man-kicks-dog game; it takes away everyone's dignity. For me, the game became an obsession, and it caused me to hurt the very people I love. The time has come for me to bury the dog. So I guess I'm sharing the message partly because I need to look at my own motives, need to look at my guilt-past and present-and partly because I want to show the reactions and ethics of local bureaucrats when their power is threatened. I know that it sounds like a sour grapes attitude. It is. But it doesn't change what happened. The grapes really were sour-and I haven't spit them out yet.

I am writing this not only to share a message, but also to share an adventure: the adventure of finding myself again by repeating the simple Twelve Steps taught to me years ago. Those steps had relieved me of the madness created by drinking alcohol. When I found that I had acquired an obsession for the game of Cops and Robbers, I eventually began working the same Twelve Steps. Ultimately, I was also relieved of the obsession to the game, but only after I finally gave up and followed their simple instructions. The adventure I want to share began one morning when I walked down to my garage to put a suitcase in the trunk of my car.

# Contents

Prologue ......................................................................................vii

Chapter 1. The Bust ......................................................................1

Chapter 2. The Jail… .....................................................................12

Chapter 3. The Courtroom ...........................................................23

Chapter 4. The Defender ...............................................................28

Chapter 5. The Fox in the Henhouse ............................................34

Chapter 6. The Lawyers .................................................................41

Chapter 7. The Easter Party ...........................................................53

Chapter 8. The Anger .....................................................................62

Chapter 9. Folsom Reflections.......................................................76

Chapter 10. The Truth ...................................................................88

Chapter 11. Sanity….......................................................................98

Chapter 12. Minimum Security......................................................110

Chapter 13. The Call… ..................................................................114

Chapter 14. A Spiritual Crisis .......................................................122

Chapter 15. The Tough Road to Sanity.........................................129

Chapter 16. The Trial ....................................................................135

Chapter 17. Release .......................................................................145

Epilogue .......................................................................................156

# CHAPTER 1

# The Bust

*San Francisco Bay Area, California, January, 1984:* I rolled over and looked at the red numbers on the clock by the side of the bed. 4:06 a.m "Christ, I'm wide awake!" I thought with disgust. "Either I have to go to bed later or start my work day at 6:00" I had tossed all night over that Monterey situation last month. I wish I could forget it. After all, the judge tossed the whole thing out at the preliminary hearing. He said there was no criminal intent on my part and he was right, even though he was far from thrilled about my attitude toward doing business. So why did I keep feeling so uncomfortable? How could I have been so stupid as to let things get away from me like that? I always seem to be talking when I should have been listening. The call came from the police investigator in Monterey in June 1983, about six months earlier. I was in my Sacramento office when the secretary put him through. He was pleasant enough, but I was busy and grouchy. He said that the manager of my company's condominiums in Monterey had taken deposits from two prospective buyers amounting to $2,000 and had refused to refund them when the buyers decided not to buy. I could vaguely remember some dispute, but I couldn't remember the reason. We had been working with real estate projects with a sales value of approximately $50,000,000, not only in California, but in Hawaii, and there were 50,000,000 details to think about. In 1983

1

interest rates and inflation were double-digit, and just remaining in business was a major miracle.

Any reasonable person knowing there was a police detective on the other end of the line just doing his job would have given him assurances of full cooperation, completed the conversation, and made sure that the dispute was settled to everyone's satisfaction. Right then. But being reasonable was never my long suit, so I didn't say anything to him; I just wanted to get him off the phone so I could finish whatever I was doing. He kept talking. I finally lost patience and said to him, with more than a little agitation, "Let me ask you something. When in the hell did the Monterey Police Department start becoming a collection agency? Give me your phone number and I'll look into it and have my attorney get back to you." I knew I had created the effect I was looking for. He was so flabbergasted that he could hardly remember his own phone number.

"Well, the hell with him." I thought. "If he wants to go into the collection agency business then he'd better get used to being treated like a collection agent." I put the phone number in my briefcase, thinking I would give it to our attorney the next time I saw him, and promptly forgot the whole matter.

Two months later, in August 1983, three police cars showed up at our office with a warrant for my arrest for grand theft of $2,000 from the buyers in Monterey. I was away on a business trip at the time, so I wasn't taken into custody. When I returned, everyone was excited and couldn't wait to tell me all the details. It was so theatrical. I knew I had done nothing. I was irritated; I found it hard to believe that a law enforcement officer would use his position and arrest someone over his damaged feelings. Three police cars! Who did they think I was, John Dillinger? I decided to let my attorney handle it.

Fred, the company attorney, —a great friend-surrendered me to the court in Monterey the next week. I was released immediately on bail. A preliminary hearing was held in December 1983. The judge ruled there was no criminal intent on my part, so I should not be tried for any crime. The police detective was in the courtroom. He was very unhappy about how things turned out. No, he wasn't unhappy; he was beside himself with anger. As we left the courtroom I gave him a short version of the Bronx cheer, which did not help his disposition. I was pretty sure it was not the end of that little drama. That feeling was haunting me now in the early hours of the morning. Was I feeling the rustling of the leaves before the storm?

Now, forty-five days later, I am sure my discomfort was all just an overreaction to being arrested for the first time in my life. "I think I'm going to sell everything this year and go into something other than real estate," I thought. "I don't like being called a criminal." I never dreamed being arrested would affect me that way. At least I didn't have to spend any time in jail. I thought I'd go have some breakfast. I was certainly not going back to sleep.

The breakfast was terrible. When I returned, the condominium parking lot was full. "The Bay Area is becoming overpopulated," I thought. "I'll be glad to get home." As I thought of going home, I saw a car with my home town TV station call letters parked in the lot. I wondered what they were doing so far from home.

It was 6:00 A.M. I was to meet Fred at 8:30 to sign papers on the escrow, but I felt like going home. I expected Fred to be irritated, but he could handle things without me, and I had plenty to do at the office, so it was not as if I'd be wasting the day. I called Ginger and asked her to meet me. I took the suitcase down to the car, intending to call Fred to cancel our appointment.

As I opened the trunk I noticed that the garage door was open. I heard the roar of an automobile and the screeching of brakes. I turned to see a police car blocking the entrance to the garage. A policeman emerged, looking terribly grim. "Wow! What's going on?" I thought. "I'm in the middle of a drug bust." I walked over to the police car and asked what was going on and received a very unfriendly, "I don't know."

Fortunately, it was not a drug bust. Some trigger-happy drug dealer might have started shooting and I probably would have been caught in a crossfire. The cop wouldn't have had time to worry about me and would have protected himself.

But they were not after a drug dealer. Mrs. Costanzo didn't raise the smartest of boys, I would be first to admit, but she did teach me how to add two and two. I glanced over the top of the police car and saw a man holding a TV camera marked with the TV call letters of my hometown; I remembered the car in the parking lot, added that I was very uneasy about being aquitted in Monterey last month and quickly came up with an answer that added to four. They're not here on a drug bust. They were here to bust me.

My first thought was to contact Fred. I needed my attorney. No, it wasn't my first thought; it was my only thought. I ran out of the garage as fast as my legs would carry me and headed for the condo with a posse of police following on my heels, shouting for me to stop, threatening to shoot, cursing extremely loud obscenities, but I was not to be denied. I breezed into the house well ahead of my pursuers. Call Fred, that's what I must do at all costs! Even if they kill me.

"Open the door, it's the police!"

Bang-bang-bang!? Fred, there is a whole army outside my door waiting to arrest me! Get over here quick."

"Are you kidding me, Frank? It's six forty-five in the morning and much too early for jokes. I haven't even had my coffee yet." I held the phone out toward the door so he could hear the shouting and pounding and said, "Goddamn it, does that sound like a joke? Get over here right away. I have to go open the door and let them in before they knock it down."

I walked down the hall quite calmly, totally ignoring the noise on the other side of the door, "There is nothing to worry about now," I thought. "I'm a citizen, I have my constitutional rights, I have an excellent attorney, and he is on his way over." I'm not sure just what I expected him to do, but I was certain that justice would prevail. At that moment I failed to realize that my idea of justice was not quite what the people on the other side of the door's definition was. I still didn't know how to play the game of Cops and Robbers; the game had not yet become an obsession.

One of the persons on the other side of the door was the Assistant District Attorney. I had very little association with those gentlemen who represent "The People." I assumed District Attorneys were like the man on the old radio show, which I listened to occasionally as a boy, called "Mr. District Attorney-Champion Of The People, Defender Of Life, Liberty, and the American way." I didn't care a lot for that show. I liked "The Shadow" much better. I realize now that D.A.'s are just lawyers. Nevertheless, I was surprised to see this Assistant D.A. was little more than a kid-in a trench coat, for heavens sake. He had a black mustache that seemed to be there to cover his adolescent features. He was very serious and reminded me of some of the characters I had seen in the old B movies where the head of the Gestapo, in his trench coat, was carrying on the house-to-house search. I was sure this Trench-Coat Kid, like his fictional Nazi counterpart, would soon ask me to sign a confession, with the understanding that he would guarantee me a quick death; if I refused to sign, he could not be responsible for the time these men would take to kill me. I had a hard time taking things seriously, even though I was sitting on the couch tightly handcuffed and he was directing the police officers to put all my files in boxes to be carted away, along with yours truly. Most of the police officers were pleasant enough, except for one who kept screaming for me to sign a piece of paper, which I refused to do. I figured he was just trying to frighten me and was probably a pretty nice person. I later learned while observing him in court that he always seemed to be angry. Especially at me. "Oh, well, Fred would know what to do," I kept telling myself.

The phone on the desk rang and one of the officers answered. He summoned the Trench-Coat Kid. I could tell by listening to the Kid's conversation that Fred was demanding to see me immediately. My trench-coated friend promptly refused. After the telephone conversation they all smiled at one another knowingly of some little secret they all shared to which I wasn't privy, so I began to conclude that these people had little interest in what my attorney might say. I told myself to stay calm and keep a cool head, but it was becoming clear that a major storm was brewing.

I wasn't worried much, though, I had never been busted before, but I've seen enough television to know that these guys were doing everything wrong. If they kept this up I'd be able to sue them for every penny they or the County had. First, they didn't read me my rights. Now everyone knows they have to read you your rights. Isn't that right? Wrong! Later, when I told Fred this great news, he sighed that sigh that attorneys sigh when their clients are telling them how to practice law and told me they didn't have to read me my rights under these conditions for some reason I never did quite understand. I accepted his explanation at face value, although I grumbled a lot. My opinion, which didn't count for much through the whole adventure, was that we should take this matter directly to the Supreme Court. I tend to become very emotional at times. Luckily I had someone like Fred to keep some semblance of order in this adventure.

Their next mistake was that they took all my files, not only the ones listed on the search warrant. They even took my correspondence with Fred. By the time we were able to have the issue of attorney-client privilege heard in court, I was feeling differently about my position as an accused felon. By that time almost one and one-half years had gone by and I had become accustomed to losing. We lost. I never asked anyone why.

The last thing they did wrong was not to let me speak with my attorney. Even though the young man in the trench coat testified it would have been too difficult to secure the area so Fred could speak with me alone, I'm quite sure I would have been able to charge him with a misdemeanor, but there was enough madness yet to happen. I didn't need to add to the chaos by bringing criminal charges against the Trench-Coat Kid. There were times during all the litigation that the idea sounded tempting though. I left the condo about three hours later, under guard, with crowds of people staring and television cameras spinning. I was tired from all the emotion and the lack of sleep. The police put me in the front seat of the car. Directly behind me was a man who said he had a .357 magnum and would blow my head off if I tried anything. I thought he was needlessly melodramatic, but you have to admit he had a good hand to bluff with. I decided not to try anything, although I couldn't for the life of me think of anything to try even if I had wanted to.

They brought me to the parking lot of a small police substation, where Fred was standing waiting for me. I no longer had the feeling I had just a few hours earlier- that Fred could fix everything-but it was good to see a friendly face. I gave him a hug when we met. That's when I realized what the guy in the back seat meant when he talked about trying anything. It really shook him. I still didn't understand the rules of the game, but I realized then that cops and robbers don't hug much. I convinced him that was how I greet all my good friends and it was no reason for blowing my head off. He acquiesced reluctantly. They told us they had no place for us to meet in the substation but we could talk in Fred's car after I submitted to a search. I submitted, and Fred and I were able to talk alone for the first time.

I asked him what I was charged with and he told me he didn't know and no one would tell him. How's that for a confidence builder? I said, with a slight tinge of sarcasm, "Fred, I have complete confidence in your ability to defend me. I'm certain that as soon as someone tells us why I've been arrested and why they have ransacked my apartment you will do something useful and get about the business of defending." Even though it was sarcastic, that statement sounded about as rational as any of the morning's events. Fred gave me the impatient frown that he puts on when I become particularly obnoxious. I apologized and the frown went away. I was becoming a little irritated, probably because I was tired, so I decided to stay calm and do exactly what Fred advised. Fred told me to waive through, whatever that meant, and he would meet me in my hometown that afternoon. I told him, "Please make sure because it is Friday and there's a three day weekend coming up. I certainly don't want to be sitting in some jail until next Tuesday before we get into a courtroom." He promised he would.

As they led me into the substation I kept glancing back, watching Fred talk to the Trench-Coat Kid. Just as I turned the corner to go into the building I saw Fred waving his arms almost hysterically. Something was definitely wrong. I turned to the guard and told him I had forgotten to ask my attorney an important question and could I return for just a minute? He agreed but warned me not to hug again. We returned to the parking lot. Fred was ashen. After they had taken me away they had served him with search warrants for his residence and office and told him he was a suspect, although no charges had been filed. I was sure they had to be kidding! Fred was the most ethical attorney I had ever met. I had always valued my relationship with him. His conservative advice offset my natural tendencies to move too fast and to make rash decisions. How could they possibly suggest that an attorney of Fred's stature would do something illegal?

The policeman was becoming somewhat irritated, so considering that .357 magnum he still had in his holster, I didn't want him to have even the slightest feeling that I was "trying anything." Being new at the game of Cops and Robbers, I thought I should be extra careful until I got my feet on the ground. I told him I was finished and he could take me away. It was becoming pretty apparent that Mrs. Costanzo's boy had a lot of problems that were not going to be solved that day or any day in the near future; that I probably would not see Fred today and would spend my three day holiday lounging around some jail cell.

I was born into a family that had strong Italian traditions. Even though I was not full-blooded Italian, that was the culture I lived in. I was taught from earliest childhood certain truths, most of which were based on love, honor and family. These truths for the most part established for me a very good life and, hopefully, a good life for my family no matter what the conditions, good or bad. Some of these truths were utterly ridiculous, but being the good young Italian boy I was, I never questioned that I was not being told the absolute truth. I believed that those truths had been dictated directly to my adult family members by whatever God there was in the heavens above.

The first indication that there was a slight possibility that some of these truths should be taken with a grain of salt was revealed to me shortly after my wife and I married. We were only nineteen at the time, and we first settled in a small town called Grass Valley, in the foothills of the Sierras in Northern California. We had a very small apartment with no television or radio. Of course, when you're first married these items, seemingly indispensable in today's world, have a very low priority. At least they did for us.

I was working in the logging camps at the time. It was hot, heavy, dirty work, and I would come home dirty from head to foot and starving to death. I would wash my hands and face, then sit down and eat everything on the table but the tablecloth. When dinner was over I did a very strange thing. I would carefully spread the last night's paper over the couch, then sit down and read the current edition. My new wife watched this ritual for about a week and finally said, "Honey, why don't you go in and take your bath first so you can sit and read the paper clean and comfortable?"

I looked up and casually remarked, "I would but I can't take a bath for an hour after I eat." She looked at me curiously, trying to figure out whether I was really serious. When she realized that I was, she broke into hysterical laughter. I looked at her with some irritation, then it hit me what a stupid remark I had just made. What could possibly happen? Would this big strapping logger get cramps and drown? That was unlikely. I began to laugh, and the incident has remained a family joke.

I began looking at that incident and started to realize that when I was young someone had told me not to take a bath for an hour after I ate. I never questioned its credibility. For me it was the truth. I tried to become aware of a lot of the untrue truths I believed. One of these was that a good Italian father protected his family and honor by any and all means, never calculating the eventual consequences to everyone involved. I don't mean to imply that all Italian men feel this way, as I would imagine most are able to take a bath less than an hour after they eat, but for me that was a truth that I was able to recognize as an untruth. I had always felt I had left that untrue truth behind me many years ago. I felt that way until the afternoon of the day I was busted.

I was taken from the substation to the local county jail by my .357 magnum-packing friend and a driver who was very pleasant. I never did see the gun, and now that I am a bit more familiar with the game of Cops and Robbers, I doubt he actually carried such a high-powered weapon. He certainly made his point, though, and he had little to fear from me. It was about lunchtime, so they decided to have lunch while I waited in a holding cell. They said they would return shortly and escort me to the jail in my hometown. I later realized they were also delaying my arrival in my hometown until all the courts had closed for the weekend so I would have to wait until the following Tuesday before getting a shot at making bail. Since Fred was being subjected to a search that would effectively block any chance of his making it. I had little chance of being arraigned that day under any conditions. Score one for the Trench-Coat Kid! I was receiving my first real lessons on how to play the game.

At the jail I asked to use a telephone. I phoned my office and received no answer. That seemed odd, so I phoned home hesitantly. I didn't want to upset anyone. I believed Fred was the only one who knew anything about this morning's events, and he had problems of his own and probably would not have had time to inform my family. My daughter answered. She was very upset. She explained that the police had come to the house early that morning with a search warrent and forced her, her son, and the housekeeper to remain in the front room while they searched the house. She told me that the police had raided my offices and carted away all the files and had raided my son-in-law's law offices and took all his files that had to do with the company or the family. Then she broke down and sobbed. She said that they had arrested my wife! Those dirty sons-of-bitches! Why would they do that? Ginger is an artist, a housewife, a loving mother, a wonderful wife, but she had no connection with my business.

As I returned to the holding cell I suddenly lost my sense of humor and along with that, my sense of proportion. The old untrue truth kicked in: I once again believed that men like me protected their families and honor no matter what the cost. I decided to fight, but false pride and the desire for revenge are very costly emotions. Because of the seriousness of the events unfolding, I owed it to my family and to myself not to bring those two emotions into play, but I was consumed with the thought of striking back and made a conscious decision to fight-and my family suffered for that decision. Once again I had failed to heed the rustling of the leaves that began in Monterey. The wind was increasing. The storm was moving slowly over the horizon. Pride and revenge were about to catapult me into obsession.

# CHAPTER 2

# *The Jail...*

We arrived at the Jail just a few minutes after 5:00 p.m. The two officers assigned to drive me from the Bay Area had been courteous and pleasant enough. I didn't try anything and no one blew my head off. It seemed to be a pretty good trade-off; I have unusual acumen with a gun to my head. They brought me to a window and the booking officer looked at me and said, "Oh, you brought the star. His new television program ended a few minutes ago, but they have a series running about his exploits all next week on Channel 3 News." I had no clue as to what he was talking about, but I was very tired and thought, "Swell, just what I need right now is a joker!"

Since I had never been in jail before I wasn't sure what to expect, but I shouldn't have been apprehensive. There is really nothing to it. I mean that literally. If you know how to do nothing, you have it made. I've known how to hang around since I was a kid growing up on the streets with my friends, watching good-looking girls and good-looking cars. We hung around pool halls, barbershops, boys clubs, girls houses and each others houses, lying to each other about how macho we were or how great we were with girls. None of us ever listened to the others; we just waited our turn so we could tell our own lies. That experience equipped me for jail, which was a series of days hanging around. I just needed to brush up on my skills.

The jail routine was calculated to degrade the inmates because a man who doesn't feel good about himself is easier to deal with. Hanging around, bitching about the food and the lousy living conditions is safer than talking about escape or riot. Actually, I found that I could overcome most of the degrading hurdles easily in the first day or two because I didn't take it all too seriously. I was put in a large holding cell with several other men, where I crossed the first major hurdle. The toilets are placed conspicuously in the room, out in the open, leaving the user absolutely no privacy. Out of necessity, I adjusted to the inevitable and hardly gave privacy a second thought again.

Another minor irritation occurred when I was being issued clothing and bedding before being transferred upstairs to a jail tank that would be my living quarters for the next few days. I was strip-searched for the first time. I had to bend over, spread my cheeks, and cough. I asked the guy next to me why they made us do that, and he looked at me in total disbelief. I'm sure it never occurred to him that anyone would not know that there are people living in these institutions who smuggle in dope in balloons up their rectum. After he explained things, I realized immediately that I had asked a very obvious and foolish question and tried to recover by saying, "Oh yeah! I forgot!" He smiled at me, and with all the compassion anyone can muster in a place like that, he said, "Take it easy, Pops, it won't take long for you to pick up what's happening." Pops! Now that was the ultimate degradation. I was forty-eight years old and in much better shape than those damn kids. It took me quite a while to become used to that "handle." The fact was that in jail, forty-eight years old to most inmates was bordering on the age of Methuselah.

I turned in my clothes and received some loosely fitting black sweat-pants and a yellow sweatshirt, two pairs of underwear, slippers, two pairs of socks, a toothbrush, a comb, a paper-thin mattress, one sheet, and two wool blankets. I looked pretty ridiculous, but I didn't care; it was now 9:30 p.m. and I had passed the point of being tired and was on the brink of exhaustion. I had been awake since four o'clock that morning. A lot had happened that day and I really didn't care what I looked like or what they did to me as long as I could find a place to lie down on this stupid thin mattress and go to sleep.

The guards crowded us all into a large elevator and made us stand facing the back wall. A guard started explaining, in a very loud voice, some very rigid rules they expected us to follow. It had been a long day of people ordering me around and I just didn't give a damn for his rules. What could he do if I didn't obey his rules, arrest me? I found that jail guards become ineffective unless they back up their talk with the threat of violence. The threat is always there, and some do use violence, but that's not the rule, no matter what we see in the movies. Once someone takes your freedom, he has really done about as much as he can do to you. Being slightly roughed up, more bad food, extra-bad living conditions, loss of visitation rights, and the like, are puny punishments in comparison to the loss of the right to live with your loved ones and to function within society.

The guards opened the door. I entered the first jail tank I had ever seen. I was immediately rocked back by the noise. A television set was braced about six feet up on the back wall, tuned to a rock video station, with the volume turned up as high as it would go. The tanks on either side had their televisions tuned to video stations with the volume turned up to exactly the same level. People were talking as loud as they could so they could be heard over the television noise. It was so loud that it was difficult to distinguish specific sounds; there was just noise.

The tank was a large concrete room with iron bars across the front, divided down the middle by another row of iron bars. Through the dividing bars I could see bunks stacked two high; an open door to my left provided access to that part of the tank. I was standing in the day room, such as it was, which contained two metal tables, the toilet underneath the television with someone sitting on it, a washbasin and a portable shower. All the conveniences of home. I searched around to find someone who looked as though he had some semblance of sanity, but the only one that seemed to have his wits about him was sitting on the toilet. In all this bedlam he looked peaceful and serene, oblivious to the fact that most eyes were focused on the television set directly above him. I decided not to bother him. It was obvious that his apparent contentment comes only occasionally in this atmosphere.

I stood there, holding my few meager possessions-mattress, blankets, and so on, when someone took pity on me and yelled, "Hello, Pops!" It was nice to hear a friendly voice, even if it was shouting and addressing me by a name I found somewhat repugnant. I inquired as to which bunk was mine and from the expression on his face I realized I had, again, made a stupid remark. He told me in a gentle but screaming voice that this was a twelve-man tank and I was the eighteenth man to be housed there that night. Since there were eighteen men and twelve beds, and since I was the bottom man on the totem pole, I was more than welcome to lay my mattress down anywhere on the concrete floor where I could find some space. Even the tops of the tables had been spoken for.

I went through the door into the area containing the bunks and laid my mattress out near the front bars, which was a mistake because it was the middle of winter and a cold wind was whipping down the corridor. I was cold, but I didn't care; I put the sheet over the mattress, rolled up one blanket as a pillow, lay down, pulled the other blanket over me, and went to sleep.

Well, some days just seem to be better than others, and this one had been zero on a scale of one to ten. I figured it was best just to go to sleep, wake up tomorrow morning, and see if I might be able to change my luck.

I am always amazed at what just a little sleep does for my attitude. Although they woke us at 4:00 a.m. for breakfast, I felt well rested even though I was somewhat blue from the cold. The breakfast was mostly junk food, so I traded most of it for additional oatmeal and an extra cup of coffee. The lights went off again for two more hours. That was when the rest of the tank went to sleep after having been awake all night.

It was absolutely quiet, so I crawled under the blanket and tried to meditate. I tried to focus on Ginger and hoped that she was handling all of this well. I love her very much and I tried to keep my feelings about revenge in check. Now was the time to try to transmit loving and caring thoughts to her. I believe I succeeded. I looked out from under the blanket at the sleeping tank. Being here seemed unbelievable but I tried to keep in my mind that I have a good life-much, much better than most. I have someone I love and who loves me, I have five wonderful children and a stepdaughter who are all healthy and also love me, I do not use drugs, alcohol, or nicotine, I have excellent health, good relatives and friends and a reasonable education. It's easy to accept adversity under those conditions.

The day went well. It took a little doing but I was able to use the telephone and I reached my son at home. He had talked to Ginger; she was doing well and in good spirits. That alone made my day. He told me bail was $150,000 on each of us, and Fred was arranging a bail reduction hearing on Tuesday. I told him to do whatever was necessary to put up bail for his mother. He told me to relax, that friends and relatives were arriving at the house in droves. The television program that featured me was seen all the way to the Bay Area. Ginger's cousin, Rick, who is terribly bright and whom I trust completely, was already making preliminary arrangements, but it would be difficult to do much until after the three-day weekend. I looked around that tank and was absolutely sure that no one there was receiving that kind of support from his family. I knew I truly did have a good life.

I was able to commandeer the telephone one more time. I took a chance and dialed Fred's office. He not only was in but had already started work on Tuesday's hearing. He was beside himself, he was so angry. After he had left me the police had treated him like a criminal, insisting that a police officer ride in his car from the substation to his office in San Francisco. They wouldn't even let him go to the bathroom alone. I wondered what kind of system is this that allows the police to intimidate a defense attorney? They confiscated many of his files. I thought about asking him about the law regarding attorney-client privilege but I kept quiet. Fred did not yet seem to be in the mood for that discussion.

I did find out what I was being charged with-well, sort of-for the first time. They had charged Ginger and me with seven counts of grand theft and one count of conspiracy. I asked Fred what they said I had stolen. He said the warrant didn't mention specifics. When I asked who it was I stole from, whatever I was supposed to have stolen, he mentioned seven real estate projects. I said, "Christ, Fred, my company owns or owned all of those projects under contracts of sale. How can I be stealing from myself?" He cautioned me not to fret, that we would have some answers in due course. Damned easy for him to say from a well-lighted, warm, comfortable office in San Francisco's financial district.

Fred warned me to not create any chaos over the next few days in jail, as he was trying to have the bail reduced and didn't want to deal with reports that I wasn't a model inmate. I thought that was a funny thing to say. What did he think I would do, especially here? I admit I am not a shy, retiring person, but I certainly have always felt I had good common sense. Nevertheless, before the bail reduction hearing Fred sent my son-in-law to see me. He advised me to be calm when I first saw Ginger in prison garb. I was beginning to realize that other people did not see me as I saw myself. It was apparent both my attorney and my son-in-law felt I had a volatile personality. This happened again and again during all the hearings and the trial as I listened to other people-long-term employees, associates, and even family members-give testimony about a person whom I did not recognize. I had no idea they had such deep feelings about my behavior. The experience was humbling.

I knew that Ginger must have been enduring a lot of uncertainty. My heart leapt when Ginger and I met for the first time after the arrests, outside the courtroom, both of us still in custody. They brought me down a hallway leading to the prisoners' entrance. I was tired since I had been in a holding cell since six o'clock that morning, in the middle of winter with the cell windows left wide open. I was sure she was just as tired.

Ginger came down the hall looking as if she were going to a costume party wearing a very camp costume. She had on a bright yellow sweatshirt with "Sacramento County Jail" stamped over the front, black baggy pants, and some silly-looking slippers. She was absolutely beautiful. She was the most beautiful woman I had ever met, and I have believed that from the day I met her. I tried not to laugh but I couldn't help myself. She frowned for just a moment and began to laugh, too. I had forgotten that I was dressed the same way. For some reason, the guards let us alone, so we kissed. She said, "Goddamn it, Honey, sometimes living with you is a pain in the rear." That wasn't a joke. We both assumed we would do anything for each other, but sometimes I think I require more from a woman than most men do.

When we stopped giggling, I asked her how she was getting along. She said things were fine, under the circumstances. When she was brought to the jail they asked her to sign a statement, but she refused without first speaking to Fred. So they put her in a solitary confinement cell for the next couple of days. I would assume, now having a bit more knowledge of the game of Cops and Robbers, they thought that after a while she would sign anything just to get out of solitary. She said that it was like a vacation. Someone got her some paper and pencils. She spent the time drawing. She was working on certain drawings that she had been thinking about but had never had the time to experiment with at home. I had to laugh to myself. She discovered the same thing I had: no one can put you in a jail but yourself. If you feel you are locked up, you are. In or out of jails.

When it became obvious that Ginger wasn't going to break down, they released her to a dormitory. Once the young girls in her dormitory discovered she could draw, she began to draw portraits of their boyfriends from photographs. The girls then took care of all her needs.

I sighed and wondered why was I so worried about this amazing woman, who had never conceived of ever seeing the inside of a jail under any circumstances, who with no warning had been scooped off the street, put in a jail in solitary confinement, then reacted as though this was just an irritation rather than a catastrophe. Did I mention that I love her?

We held hands and were led through the door into the busy courtroom. Television cameras were whirling, a frowning judge was directly above us, Fred and John, Ginger's new attorney, were moving across the room toward us, the Trench-Coat Kid, minus the trench coat, sat seriously stroking his mustache, family members were out there crying. I leaned over and gave Ginger a quick kiss. I was hoping that the guy with the .357 magnum wasn't there because I was pretty sure he had very little romance in his soul. If he had been there, kissing in a courtroom might have pulled him out of his chair, gun blazing. No one shot me, so I guess he wasn't in the courtroom or I had simply misjudged his feelings about romance. Most likely he just wasn't there. I'm sure I had pegged him correctly on the romance issue. The judge continued to frown. He didn't seem to have much romance in his soul, either.

As we separated in the hall after leaving the courtroom, Ginger turned as they were leading her away and said in a sultry voice. "Hey, big boy! If you need anything, just whistle."

I was not released on bail that Tuesday, as I had anticipated, but on the Monday following the Tuesday hearing. The Tuesday bail reduction hearing had been postponed until the following Friday afternoon and at that time Ginger's bail was reduced to $25,000 and mine was reduced to $100,000. By late afternoon after the hearing on Friday, the best they could do was arrange the paperwork for Ginger. She was released that evening. After hearing the news I sighed a big sigh of relief.

My stay in our cozy little tank was uneventful, but I began to hone my hanging-around skills, hoping I would not need them again. For the most part, everyone was a dope addict or alcoholic whose crimes were directly related to their addiction, mostly burglaries committed to raise the funds needed to feed their habit. Waiting to be turned over to the federal authorities were a couple of Mexican dope dealers who couldn't speak English and kept to themselves: there was one person who was accused of shooting a cop but swore he couldn't remember because he was in an alcoholic blackout. There was always dope being passed around. I just turned away because I did not want to have anything to do with it, and I wanted to make sure I had no idea where it came from. You didn't have to be a mental giant to figure out that the less you knew, the better off you were.

I knew right from the beginning that I would need to deal with the noise problem and easily did so. I'm aware that noise is only in my mind. If I decide not to hear it, I don't. The television was on constantly, from early morning to the time the guards turned it off at night. I stayed up after the 4:00 a.m. breakfast to meditate and clean the floor area where I slept. The tank was unbelievably dirty, but I certainly had no intention of living like that. I kept my living area spotlessly clean. Except for the televisions, it was relatively quiet during the day, because most of the inmates, who had been up all night, were asleep. Because I was up so early, I usually went to sleep at 8:30 in the evening. In this way I subjected myself to very little of the madness I experienced my first evening.

No matter what was happening, every evening at five o'clock everything would stop for the Channel 3 News. Channel 3 was running a daily series on my multimillion-dollar exploits. It was a bit melodramatic. I wondered how they had accumulated so much information when I didn't even know I was being investigated. It crossed my mind a few times while watching the mini-documentary that they had made no attempt to contact me to see whether there was another side to the story. Just as well, though; I probably would have thrown them out. They labeled me the "Criminal of the Eighties." My God, they must have been on the same dope my tankmates were. That statement was as outlandish as anything I heard in the tank.

Every one of my tankmates was duly impressed and it wasn't worth trying to deny the charges. They weren't familiar with the old adage not to believe everything you hear on the news and they were most happy to have what they thought was a heavy hitter like me sharing their tank. With all their plaudits, however, not one of them offered me his bunk. This old heavy hitter continued to spend his nights sleeping on the concrete. For some reason the Mexican dope dealer gave me a warm blanket. I had no idea why he performed such a compassionate act; I didn't understand a word he said, and all we had done was exchange smiles. There is a time to take the gifts God puts in your life and accept them graciously. I certainly didn't turn it down.

I was transferred from downtown to a facility called The Ranch just outside of the city. The only similarity it had to a ranch was that it was located outside the metropolitan area. Otherwise, it looked exactly like what it is: a jail, complete with guard towers, chain-link fences, and barbed wire. It was noisy, but I could look out a window. I even had a bunk. Two hours after I arrived, I was lying on a real bed for the first time since I was arrested. My name was called over the loudspeaker for me to get ready to be released. Get ready? What a laugh! I had been ready for eleven days. Just open the door and I'll be history. When they took me outside there was a great deal of confusion because my street clothes had not yet been sent from downtown. They took away all my prison clothes. I stood around naked in the cold for about forty-five minutes. Finally a guard threw me a sweatsuit, told me to put it on and get out. I was confused because I knew the county wouldn't let me leave with such an expensive outfit, but I climbed into the sweatpants and was still putting on the sweatshirt as I ran through the door. I saw Ginger's cousin, Rick, wave to me from the car. I looked in the back seat as I got in and saw his brother,

Randy, sitting there in his shorts. I realized that the sweatsuit was Randy's. He had sat around in front of a jail with no clothes on to make sure I got out that night rather than make me wait until the following morning.

# CHAPTER 3

# The Courtroom

Six and one-half months later, in August of 1984, the temperatures were hovering around the 100 degree mark. Ginger and I were driving to the courthouse to begin a hearing on misconduct by the police and the Trench-Coat Kid, to be followed by the preliminary hearing. In most cases the preliminary hearing is a simple legal procedure where the District Attorney puts on just enough evidence to show that the defendant might have committed the crime he is accused of and therefore should stand trial. Ginger was saying she was glad to get started so we could finish it all and get on with our lives. I thought lovingly, "My God, how innocent her thinking is. Even about me." We had started going together when we were fourteen and married when we had just turned nineteen, so we had been together at that time for more than thirty-five years. She not only loves me but she thinks I'm as innocent as she is. I've been a promoter for most of our married life and have fought many battles, only she was never aware of them. She was taking care of our family. She trusted me. I thought that's why it's so important to be careful until she is out of it. Then I'll hit them with both barrels. My obsession with the game of Cops and Robbers was growing.

I was feeling wound up and could see myself beginning to enjoy the game of Cops and Robbers. I've always been a player, a crapshooter in business. A professional gambler in Vegas once told me, "The next best thing to playing and winning is playing and losing." So even though I found it difficult to gamble five dollars in a casino, I had always been addicted to games that would pit my will against others. After all, this particular game was nothing more than a game of egos. I'd certainly match my ego against anyone's. The egos on the other side were being financed by the taxpayers while I had to bankroll myself. Still, things were fairly even, because I felt I was smarter than they were. Of course, the stakes were high enough: prison. I realized deep down that I didn't really have enough chips to play-but the game was just too fascinating to pass by.

They had charged us with eight felony counts, including recharging me with the old Monterey case in which I had already been acquitted. I must have asked Fred the question about double jeopardy a thousand times. As usual, I did not receive an understandable answer. It became obvious that a person can be charged for the same crime twice. It was, after all, happening to me-but I was becoming tired of demanding we go directly to the Supreme Court with no one paying the slightest attention. The charges carried a maximum sentence of eleven and one-half years but who was counting? Eleven and one-half years is a sobering thought, but the will to fight or the desire to play was much stronger. The obsession had me now. In my mind I was innocent of the charges; but as I reflect, even if I was innocent under the letter of the law I probably was guilty under the spirit of the law.

Fred figured it was going to be just another day in court. I knew it wouldn't because I was going to do everything in my power to turn it into a circus. This was my first real chance to be heard since they arrested us. I was mad. I was determined to make life as uncomfortable as I could for these guys. I figured this case would have the same type of ending as the Rocky movies. They would beat me up real good, and I would try to do the same to them. Victory would depend on who was standing when the bell rang after fifteen rounds.

We went directly to the courtroom where Fred, who was driving up from San Francisco, said he would meet us. We had hired John, a top local criminal attorney to defend Ginger. I had known John for many years but never had the need for his services before, as he specialized in criminal work. I had great respect for him as an attorney and as a human being. This was important because we were depending on him to show the court exactly how little Ginger knew about the business.

John's courtroom personality was taken from a Spencer Tracy movie. He always tried to leave the impression that he was just a good old boy, fumbling around, distracting the listener's attention with a million stories; then slamming home a direct question designed to get to the truth in an unguarded moment. His mind was uncluttered, always knowing where he wanted to be at the end rather than becoming bogged down with all the details of getting there. He was thoughtful and tough but compassionate within the limits that a criminal attorney allows himself without emotional involvement. I regarded him as a real friend, but I was absolutely sure he would sell my soul to the Devil in Hell, if necessary, to protect Ginger. Of course, that was the job he was hired to do, and he performed it with maximum efficiency, ethically walking the line of friendship, yet dedicated to defending Ginger.

The hallway outside the courtroom was crowded. I spotted the television cameras focusing on the courtroom doors where we would enter. I knew they saw me but they made no move to rush over to us as they had in the past. That's usually a sign that something is wrong, when things don't happen the way they normally do. Fred walked up and told me that the Trench-Coat Kid had been meeting with the judge and had called a meeting of the attorneys in chambers as soon as John arrived. John was always late; he had appearances in other courtrooms for other clients going all the time.

Ginger had settled into a conversation with Fred. He was relaxed and filled with his usual banter about his one great love, music. Fred is a cellist and a magnificent singer. He always speaks with such passion about his love for music. He could discourse about music as well as he could play and sing, but today I was not very interested. I was trying to anticipate what our adversaries were going to do to catch us off guard. Eventually, John walked up and he and Fred went into the judge's chambers, presumably to discuss whatever matters attorneys feel they want to discuss before going on the record. I believed that they were very worried about Fred. He knew everything about my business, which was highly complex. He was a skilled trial attorney and a loyal friend. A couple of months back, they made a motion to have him removed as my attorney, using their theory that he was a suspect in the case. The judge had thrown out their motion, and all they accomplished was to make him more determined to fight along with me. He had come after them like a whirlwind, and they were now faced with the prospect of defending their own conduct. Their conduct had been something less than exemplary as they had been using my son-in-law, who was a former attorney for the family and the company, as an informer. I was certain he felt justified in what he had done and we all do what we feel we need to do in this life. I certainly had no hard feelings after I recovered from the initial shock. The infuriating part was that, after the arrests were made, that information was kept secret. He visited me in jail to ask questions and then met with Fred and discussed the case, giving Fred the impression he wanted to be a part of the defense team. No one ever revealed that he was the prosecution's informant. The situation with my son-in-law was truly a dilemma. Ginger and I love our daughter and our grandchildren dearly. My daughter loved her husband and would never believe he would be an informer against her mother and father. I really admired that quality in her. I have always felt that when a daughter marries, her first obligation is to her spouse, if at all possible, not to her family. I think that is one of the real truths I learned as a boy.

I intuitively knew right from the moment I spoke with him the night I was released from jail that he was involved in some way. Ginger told me that night that she and her mother had talked and had arrived at the same conclusion. He denied it, of course, and I spent many sleepless nights agonizing over what I should do.

I always knew the proper course was to instruct the attorneys to try and make a deal where I would plead guilty if they would release Ginger, even if I believed I was innocent. I'm sure that was the reason she was arrested in the first place. But I wasn't being very honest with myself. I knew in my heart that my chances of winning were slim to none. They had unlimited resources and, although mine were greater than most, my resources were definitely limited. Guilt or innocence had little to do with a firefight like this. A rational person should have said, "If I'm going to lose, why not just plead guilty, do the time, and leave the whole mess behind me?" But I wasn't rational. I wanted to fight. They were very unhappy about having to fight. They expected me to roll over. They were surprised that we discovered my son-in-law was a confidential informant and I was about to put him on the witness stand and probably embarrass them. They also had begun to realize that perhaps much of what he had told them was simply not true. They could see that I was about to turn what seemed at the beginning a simple case into a nightmare. I would pay for those actions down the line. Why didn't I plead guilty? False pride and anger, no question. I was obsessed. I would like to think that I also believed that I deserved the right to defend myself under the Constitution. In this particular game of Cops and Robbers, the rules that they had decided upon made my defense impossible. Adventures like this create unique decisions. Most of the time I handled them badly. I looked up from my reverie to see Fred and John coming through the courtroom doors. John was very somber and Fred was white as a sheet. He was staggering almost like a drunk coming out of a barroom. I knew instantly I was about to receive another major lesson in the game of Cops and Robbers.

# CHAPTER 4

# *The Defender*

The judge agreed to postpone the start of the proceedings for a couple of hours until we-our attorneys, Ginger and I, could decide on a course of action. We certainly had some decisions to make. The Trench-Coat Kid had walked into the judge's chambers and announced that they had decided to arrest Fred, so Fred should be removed as my attorney and the hearing put off for two weeks to give me the chance to hire a new attorney.

The four of us-Fred, John, Ginger and I-huddled together in a little room next to the courtroom cafeteria. We had seemingly only one recourse: I had to plead guilty because there were now two hostages, Ginger and Fred. Fred was almost incoherent; the thought of them arresting him had never crossed his mind. John gave me a short, lucid account of what happened in chambers. The Kid had wasted no time, gave little information, stated that Fred was to be arrested and asked that the proceedings be postponed for two weeks. Under the circumstances, the judge agreed. No one had the presence of mind to ask to see the warrant, so I had no idea how they intended to charge Fred. I was confused as to my next move. The thought of pleading guilty under these conditions seemed more than I could bear-standing in room admitting to things I didn't believe, being led out through the doors to face the television cameras before they carted me away in handcuffs, facing several years in prison; there just had to be a better way. Then I suddenly remembered the television cameras. They weren't focusing on me when I walked in. What did that mean? Could this be a set-up and they had no intention of arresting Fred? They would put so much pressure on me that I'd have no choice but to plead guilty and the television cameras would be able to film me, handcuffed and under guard, after the fact, which would make a better news story. Besides the threat to Ginger and Fred, the prosecution knew I would have no way in the world of hiring another attorney in a case this complicated and having him in court, even slightly prepared, in two weeks. If I pled guilty, I was sure that part of the deal they would offer would be not to arrest Fred, which I figured they had now intention of doing anyway. I told myself that this was a pretty far-fetched theory, even tinged with a touch of panic, but it was about all I could come up with on such short notice. Now that I felt I had a theory to explain this madness, I excused myself and took a walk to figure out my best course of action. Somehow my thoughts drifted back to Skeeter, my boyhood mentor. My father worked in the coal mines of central Colorado. Our family lived in town. During the week Dad stayed in a little company cabin near the mine, maybe thirty miles into the mountains. I often spent the week there. While my Dad was working I went hiking and fishing with Skeeter, an old retired miner who lived next door to my Dad. He was one of those true friends that occasionally come into a young boy's life and makes him feel safe and warm. Usually the gap between an old man and a young boy is very small. It widens as the boy grows older.

Skeeter not only taught me how to fish. He also shared with me many words of wisdom that stayed with me for the rest of my life. Once he told me never to say "whoa" to your horse in a mudhole, or you'll sink. Never had that saying meant so much to me as it did when I was walking down that hallway. No matter how outrageous my theory seemed to be, it was all I had. I could either quit and sink or keep moving forward. I knew exactly what I was going to do, so I thought I might as well have at it. I was determined to fight. I was locked into the obsession.

I spun around and ran back to the cafeteria, pushed the door open and asked Fred to come with me. At that moment Fred was barely functioning, not thinking. I brought him outside by the fountain. The sun had risen to midmorning height and it was extremely hot. Considering the emtion of the hour and the hot sun, we were both perspiring to the point where faint signs of sweat showed through our suits. The adrenalin was pumping thoughout my body. I sat him down and said, "Fred, if you are arrested, what will happen to your law practice besides losing some money, which can be easily replaced? Will your biggest clients desert you?"

He thought for a minute of the four or five companies besides mine that formed the nucleus of his practice. "I doubt it," he said, "They've been with me for a long time, you know."

I then asked him quietly, knowing he was under a terrible strain, "Then tell me why you can't defend me, arrest or no arrest."

His reply was almost inaudible. "What bothers me most is having to tell my wife. This will be such a blow to her. I don't want her disgraced in front of her family and friends."

I was truly touched. Here he was facing arrest, with the possibility of prison, loss of practice and license and his greatest concern was how to break the news to his wife, how difficult it would be for her to deal with it all. His dilemma made me realize why I had kept Fred as my attorney all these years. He was committed to ethics and values. He loved and cared for his family and his church. He was an artist, a cellist, who performed his music thoughout the Bay Area for free, usually going directly to rehearsals after putting in twelve and fourteen-hour days in his practice. He was truly a good friend.

That was no reason not to defend me and I told him so. It wasn't professionally valid, no matter how strongly I sympathized. He was my attorney and for both our sakes, he needed to pull himself together; we were both going down the drain in the next few minutes if we didn't work out some plan to bring some order to this situation. I reminded him that I could go to prison for over eleven years. We didn't know what they would charge Fred with, but judging from the experience with Ginger, they would charge him with at least as much. He suddenly came out of the fog he had been in for the last hour, lifted himself up to his full six-foot-four frame and said, "You're right, Frank. That isn't a good enough excuse. This whole thing took me off guard. I'm still feeling shaky, but I'm still your attorney. My first obligation is to you." The horses in that mudhole had begun moving again.

I explained to him my belief that they would not arrest him. He listened. He was not convinced. I told him I wanted him to go back in the judge's chambers and explain that I have decided to go forward, with him as my attorney, no matter whether they arrest him or not. He said,"All right, Frank, What the hell? We started this fight together and we'll finish the same way." We walked back into the courthouse, with unity and ready to meet the next onslaught of the Kid in the trenchcoat.

As Fred and John emerged from the meeting in chambers, their faces made it clear that they had not made a major impression on the old man in the black robe. He wasn't impressed. After learning what I proposed to do the Kid became terribly upset. He said that I should not be represented by an attorney who has being charged with the same crime as I was and who would become a party in the proceedings. He told the judge that the court had the authority to remove Fred as my attorney over my objection and demanded that the judge do so. The judge agreed. I was left without an attorney.

I have never figured out how the judge reconciled in his mind that I was better off without an attorney than with an attorney who was facing arrest. That's why I enjoyed playing the game of Cops and Robbers. The rules always seemed to change and you had to stay at the table so they would deal you the next hand. I was sure they were making up the rules as they went along. Nevertheless, that was the situation and I had to do something quickly or become bogged down again in Skeeter's theoretical mudhole. It looked hopeless. Even if I could raise the money for another attorney, Fred was really the only person who understood the complicated transactions revolving around this case. I could never hope to prepare anyone adequately in six months, much less two weeks. There was no question in my mind that the Kid and his superiors were aware of this. I knew I couldn't go into a courtroom unprepared with Ginger and Fred on the line. I was now convinced that Fred was not going to be arrested. The prosecution was pressing to hard to obtain a continuance of this hearing and going to extraordinary lengths to have me plead guilty. Why didn't they arrest Fred four months ago rather than wait until the day we were beginning the preliminary hearing? Nothing had changed. All the facts were the same. Nothing made sense and I was sure drawing the correct conclusion. They felt that if they went into court with my son-in-law testifying they would look foolish because this was not the open-and-shut case they had been telling the media it was. They had begun to figure out that my son-in-law had not told the truth in the first place. When he was a confidential witness, they didn't have any problems. Once he was called to testify, they weren't sure what he might say under oath. Mostly though, I believed I completely mystified them. I was a loose cannon. I was not reacting they way most accused felons react. I should be begging for mercy for my wife, for my attorney and myself. I was bringing charges against the prosecution instead.

I took an inventory of my present position. First, my wife was under arrest, my son-in-law was an informant, I was facing an eleven-year prison term, they were threatening to arrest my attorney, the judge had decided to remove that attorney, I probably couldn/t raise the money to hire another attorney on such short notice and if I could I was sure he would not be prepared in the two weeks allocated for the continuance. By God, this game of Cops and Robbers can become exciting at times. I had them right where I wanted them. All I had to do was keep pushing. I asked whether anyone had any suggestions. No one said a word. To break the silence, John jokingly said,"Well, you can always represent yourself."

"That's it. I'll represent myself!"

They were sure I wasn't playing with a full deck. Fred looked directly at me, and, in one of the few times I have ever seen him irritated, told me to please stop being flippant, that things were very grave. But I was completely serious. No judge could deny me the right to defend myself and I would then be entitled to the hearing immediately. The hearing would be required to go forward; we would find out soon enough if they really intended to arrest Fred. John was an excellent attorney and could do all the questioning. Hell, I was on a roll now. If I got lucky I could talk the court into using Fred as an advisor to help Johen with some of the technical questions. If not, I was sure I could give John almost all the help he would require. I would just go in and sit quietly, as is my custom!

I explained to the attorneys what I wanted and why. They were skeptical. You had to believe the Kid was bluffing about Fred to accept the rest of the scenario. They were not ready to believe that. They were firmly convinced that Fred would be arrested-because neither of them, to their personal credit, could believe a law enforcement agency would threaten a defense attorney with arrest just to have the defendant plead guilty and take the heat off themselves. I had no such illusions. But maybe I just wanted to fight rather than sink.

After warning me of the dangers of representing myself, Fred and John acquiesced to my request and went to the chambers to inform the judge of my decision. I was positive the Kid was going to scream about it. Sometimes the rules of the game can be changed by our side, too.

# CHAPTER 5

# The Fox in the Henhouse

Weary, I leaned against the wall in the hallway. I told myself that it must be that hot sun, not the emotional turmoil of playing the game. I cautioned myself to conserve my energy because I knew I had to keep pushing, not quit, keep giving them hell, and do something other than feel sorry for myself. I just walked over to Ginger and gave her a great big hug. Ginger had become a little pressured over the last few hours, too, and the hug I gave her helped ease the tension.

I have found that hugging is physically refreshing. I was taught to hug as a child. It was something that everyone just did. My secret is to slightly rub the other person's cheek with my beard to get their attention, wrap my arms tightly around the person, then try and relax all the muscles in my body. The relaxation at the end reduces the prospect of knocking the breath out of the huggee. The hugging habit has always served as a mini-vacation from my daily pressures.

I kept my arms around Ginger and looked down the hall at the people with the television cameras. They were still there, looking unhappy and being soothed by my old friend, the Fox. The Fox was the chief real estate fraud investigating officer for the Sheriff's Department. He received his name from John, later on in the hearing, when John made one of his familiar country-boy jokes. A technical decision was required of the judge on an irrelevant legal point, but the decision would have to be made on the conflicting testimony of the chief investigator and

Ginger. Ginger had answered all questions in a straightforward manner while the chief investigator had danced around sticky subjects, giving vague answers to direct questions, and oiled, and oozed his way through areas that showed him to be a person of less than outstanding character and ability.

At summation, John characterized the chief investigator's testimony as a reminder of the story of the farmer who one evening heard a great deal of commotion in the henhouse. Grabbing his rifle, he burst into the henhouse to find a fox, belly drooping to the floor and feathers covering his mouth. When the farmer demanded to know what had become of the chickens, the fox replied, "I opened the door to this little house because I was curious to see what was in it. When I opened the door all the chickens flew out. I figured you would be worried so I stayed around to let you know what had happened." With that John turned to the judge and quietly said, "Now, Your Honor, if you believe the chief investigator's story, then you might as well believe the fox, too." The judge believed both foxes, so we lost on the point in question-but from that moment on, I laughed every time I looked at the chief investigator, because he was actually beginning to look like a fox. It was apparent that the Fox had called the television station to come over and film my demise, expecting he would receive his fair share of the notoriety and exposure; but the television people were now becoming impatient that I hadn't pled guilty yet, as he had more than likely promised them. I was awfully sorry that I held up the Fox's budding video career; he never got the recognition he felt he deserved in this life and this bust had certainly not turned out the way he had originally planned. He thought I'd be safely tucked away in some obscure little cell by this time, and the media would be singing praises of how he had saved society from the monster who stalked the city. It seemed that fame and fortune constantly eluded the Fox. I was never seriously concerned with him as a worthy adversary because I knew a lot more about the Fox than he would ever have dreamed.

Long before our arrest, a local mortgage company had collapsed, creating the largest real estate fraud ever perpetrated in the County. It had been on the front page in the city's newspapers for months, if not years. Thousands of small investors had been bilked of their savings, and the perpetrators were still running around free. When I made the decision to fight, we made careful investigations of everyone we were dealing with. The Fox, as it turned out, had taken a leave of absence from his career as a law enforcement officer and went to work for this company selling their less-than-blue-chip product. The perpetrators, it was discovered, were his in-laws. We found that a separate company had been formed, as the house of cards was collapsing, to funnel funds out of the parent company so that special clients could have their money returned without loss. One of these special clients was the Fox's father. The Fox was questioned by the District Attorney's office, cleared of any wrongdoing, rehired as a sheriff's deputy then hired by the District Attorney's office as the chief investigating officer for the real estate fraud division. I'm sure that was a very logical decision in someone's mind. I assume the job required experience. Of course, the Fox's qualifications for the job were never submitted to the general public for their advice and consent.

People like the Fox exist in every political system, I guess, and I certainly had no intention of using any of that information. It was interesting to know but hardly relevant to my case.

The crowd in the hallway had thinned considerably since we had arrived, so it was easy to see Fred and John come back through the doors of the courtroom. Their expressions were grim and tired, especially Fred's. Who could blame him? Being busted is an exhausting experience. It takes a great deal of knowledge to be a contented accused felon. The natural tendency is to see only the negative side. Although I was certainly no professional at the game, I had always been optimistic by nature and was beginning to get the hang of it. I knew Fred would never, on his most optimistic day, understand how to become a happy camper while being a primary participant in the game of Cops and Robbers.

They didn't tell me anything about the meeting that I hadn't already guessed. The judge was furious. He thought I was nothing more than a troublemaker with one hell of a nerve to question his decision to get rid of Fred and continue the hearings for two weeks. Defending myself would make a mockery of the court's dignity. I'm sure he had a point, but it all depends on whose ox is getting gored. I was staring down the barrel at eleven years in prison, and the court could forego a little dignity to assure me the best possible chance to prove my innocence. Oh well, these minor differences are what make a good game of Cops and Robbers. I had just put in a new set of rules and canceled some rules the lawyers worked out. I had forgotten that the judge was a lawyer, too.

The Trench-Coat Kid was beside himself, but he had shot his best shot and now had to settle for the inevitable. The hearings would go on and now no one was sure what would happen. The judge agreed with the Kid that they were dealing with a maniac. I had to admit that they were probably right.

Fred told me he had asked to see a copy of his arrest warrant, but the Kid said it was not available. When Fred asked whether it had been signed by a judge, the Kid said that matter was being handled by someone else in his office, and he had not had time to check as to its status. When Fred inquired as to the nature of the charges, the Kid stated he would rather not say until the warrant was issued and the arrest was made. Fred was completely frustrated, but I wasn't. I was sure that the Kid was just stalling for time, that he didn't have a warrant and never intended to issue one for Fred. I'm sure that in the Kid's mind, I should have pled guilty by now to save Fred, and the Kid would have been kind enough to let Fred off the hook. It wasn't working out that way. The Kid needed to buy some time to regroup.

What mystified me was how a so-called respectable judge could remove Fred without seeing the warrant.

I turned and glanced down the hall just in time to see the television camera people packing their equipment, looking very disgruntled. The Fox was trying to pacify them by some encouraging remark like, "Don't worry, the good guys always win out in the end," or something equally inspiring.

I do not remember much about the few minutes we spent in the courtroom requesting that I represent myself and demanding that the hearings proceed immediately. My vision blurred, the room seemed full of people, so full they appeared to be hanging from the rafters. All the attorneys seemed to be talking at once, and I suddenly began to regret my decision. For the first time since this whole adventure began, I felt very alone. I listened to the judge tell me how I would be facing a skilled prosecutor and how the courts would make no allowance for my inexperience. He asked me whether I understood everything he had said, and I replied, "I understand what you said, Your Honor." Even though I was apprehensive, I was far from convinced that what he said was true. They had agreed to allow Fred to become my advisor and sit next to me during the hearings. John was an attorney far superior to any I had met in the District Attorney's office. I was committed to following Skeeter's advice, come what may.

After making some very ungracious remarks about my mentality, the judge stated he had no choice but to grant my request and assigned the case to a courtroom one floor above. At least I had still not pled guilty, but not having Fred as my attorney was like one of those crazy dreams where you walk around with no clothes on. I soon found that although the courts and law enforcement had underestimated my ability to play Cops and Robbers, they were about to rectify that mistake forthwith. Before the week was out I would win quite a few battles. I would also lay the foundation for losing the war.

Out in the hallway I felt much better. Ginger gave me a big hug and a kiss. I needed that. Everyone was chattering as we moved toward the elevator. One of my daughters had arrived so we had a large entourage. Everyone had his own opinion as to what we should do. At this point everyone's opinion was valid because the dignity of the court had, indeed, been violated. There were absolutely no rules that anyone could follow because the Kid, the Fox, and whoever else was involved had made the decision to threaten the safety of my defense attorney. It is a fundamental constitutional right for anyone to be represented by the counsel of his choice. Using subterfuge, they decided to abandon due process of law, and they turned themselves into little more than that dog the CPO told me about, and I was determined to kick them in the ass as hard as I could.

Fred and I had dinner back during the Monterey fiasco, and he explained to me that our modern adversary legal system was based on a medieval custom where disputes were settled by knights hired to represent each of the parties. The knights would fight a duel and the dispute would be settled according to which knight won. If what I had seen so far was an indication of the criminal justice system throughout our country, we had not progressed very far from the original jousting fields.

As we walked into the new courtroom the bailiff announced that the judge wanted to meet with the attorneys in chambers. John and I began to walk to the door but my way was blocked. The bailiff informed me in no uncertain terms that his instructions were to specifically exclude me. Fred and John explained that I was representing myself and should attend any meetings of attorneys. The bailiff said the judge would be willing to meet with Fred but I was not to be allowed in without specific permission. I told Fred not to create a scene and to go in without me. It was obvious that they were going to remove my second counsel of choice, me! I considered taking this whole thing to the Supreme Court but realized I would

probably need an attorney. At the rate I was losing them that morning, my chances of ever having an attorney again seemed remote.

# CHAPTER 6

# *The Lawyers*

Playing the game of Cops and Robbers is like playing any other game: you need a few time-outs. So I left the courtroom and walked down the hallway to catch my breath and clear my mind. Ginger and my daughter were engrossed in conversation. Their foreheads were almost touching and their tone was very serious. I had the feeling they were logically discussing the situation. Ginger tends to do  that, but logic would have been totally valueless in these circumstances. The problem with straight logic in these situations is that all the players-the judge, the Kid, the Fox, Fred, and I-were personally involved and could be counted on to make decisions based on our own self-interest or the interests of our own team. The capacity for logic and the will to survive are two different human characteristics. With the possible exception of Fred, all the other players, including me, had already proven that they would bypass logic to protect themselves.

My son, who had just arrived, was standing next to his mother, totally bewildered by all the new rules of the game that everyone had invented that morning. He certainly wasn't the only one; I'm no mental giant even when things are routine. What was happening could not be classified as routine.

This upstairs hallway was relatively free of the hustle and bustle we had experienced downstairs all morning. I glanced at my watch. It was now 11:15 a.m. I glanced through the windows of some of the other courtrooms and litigation was in process, I'm sure to the delight of all the lawyers involved.

I decided to lie down on one of the benches in the hallway, close my eyes for a minute and think good thoughts. Colorado, now that is a real good thought. Ginger and I had taken a trip there last month to take a break before all of this madness started. Colorado was the state of my birth, the land my father loved so much but was never able to find the peace that the towering mountains and rushing streams provide. The family would leave there for the jobs in California that would employ an alcoholic such as he, only to return when he was absolutely sure that this time he could go back, stop drinking and live out his life in the wilderness he so desired. He would always stay sober for about two or three months and start drinking again, then become unemployable or be forced to take some menial job that would not pay enough to support his family. We would hang around the small town for six or eight months and then would pack our belongings one more time, get on the bus and return to San Francisco where drinking was a way of life and a person was not labeled the town drunk unless he ended up a wino living in doorways around Third and Howard streets. Although my mother could barely tolerate his drinking, and they fought constantly, she was born and raised in San Francisco and was more than happy to return; leaving behind the harsh life brought on by the bitter Colorado winters.

I sat on the bank of a stream and cried a couple of times, contemplating how things would have been different had my father, like me, found a way to stop drinking and had not died of alcoholism-I'm sure his long, straight black hair would be white, but he would probably still part it up the middle like George Raft. His beard would be rough and give you a whisker burn when he would hug you. He would still love to sing. I remember him standing there casting his line across the stream, singing loudly, yet never frightening away the fish as I was always sure he would. I felt there was a kind of godliness that formed like an aura around him when he was singing, fishing, and being one with nature. All life around him, including me, would be at peace. Without alcohol in his body, he was a robust and caring person. Without booze, he would have certainly found peace and serenity.

This trip was more than a sentimental journey into my childhood memories. Over the past few years Ginger and I have come to understand that a successful relationship is a partnership of three beings: the man and the woman in union with whatever spiritual being they believe in. We had come to believe that love, that unexplained warm glow of caring, compassion, and need that even atheists and agnostics experience, develops directly from a spiritual being, the third partner. It was our active participation within that partnership of the three beings that built and maintained our love.

That partnership needs to be nurtured on a consistent basis. We have always tried to spend a lot of time together alone, even when the children were young, so that the Spirit that feeds love into our union would shine brightly.

The majestic mountains gave us the backdrop to renew our love. We visited my wonderful Italian family, shopped, and even took a tour of the new golf course. But what I enjoyed most about my trip to Colorado was that each day Ginger and I would hold hands and walk over the mountain trails together under the watchful, awesome eyes of a Crested Butte, a lion with a blue mane-sometimes talking, sometimes being quiet, most of the time smiling, and all of the time loving each other. All three members of the marriage partnership were there; Ginger, I, and our own spiritual being.

We needed that third partner to help us make a major decision in our lives. The Kid had offered a deal. If I pled guilty they would let Ginger out of it. God, it reminded me of those old B movies were the Gestapo would hold a gun to the head of the prisoner's wife and then tell him if he would sign the confession they would release her; otherwise they would shoot her.

Both attorneys had advised against pleading guilty because they were certain Ginger would be released anyway. That was certainly easy for them to say. I knew deep down that I was not honest. That there was no decision to make. I should have simply pled guilty. I told myself I was being honest. I even quoted Shakespeare saying "To thine own self be true." One of the subtleties of the game of Cops and Robbers is that it makes it difficult to determine exactly what is or isn't the truth. Ginger and I finally agreed that we would make an assessment of the situation each day at the hearings. If we thought things were starting to become more than we could handle, I would plead guilty and extricate her from the whole thing. I lied, however, because I had already made up my mind to fight, and Ginger's safety was being compromised. The game had drawn me in so far that I couldn't hear the message being spoken by our third partner although it didn't appear that way.

I woke with a start and realized I had been dreaming. I dreamed of the trip Ginger and I took to Colorado last month, but couldn't put my finger on why I was so uncomfortable. The dream had something to do with Ginger, and it had begun on a positive note but soon deteriorated into an uncomfortable feeling so strong it woke me. I was sweating although the hallway was somewhat chilly. My first reaction was to pass it off as apprehension over what had happened that day, but by my age you learn, over the years, to recognize certain subtle signals from your mind and body that you had better heed or you are soon in a world of hurt: cold sweats, a lump directly in the solar plexus, shakes from too little to eat, and just having the feeling that something is missing but you don't know what. That's the time to stop and take a second look at the current situation. I tried to concentrate. The situation seemed to be about the same now as it had been in the downstairs courtroom-maybe even a little worse, if anything, considering the hostility of this new judge. Or was it the same? Nothing seemed to have changed. But I felt a difference.

Everyone, I think, has feelings of impending doom at one time or another. The trick is to understand their exact nature. Most of my life I've been pretty good at getting to the heart of a problem. But the game of Cops and Robbers had begun to wear me down that day. I had complete confidence in my ability to play the game, but that confidence was only my ego coupled with my taste for bravado. I just didn't have the experience to make the necessary decisions, and subconsciously I think I knew it. I still had my instinctive ability to react, but the truth was I was becoming scared and wouldn't admit it to myself. The Kid's strategy-bringing me into court without the attorney of my choice-had worked perfectly. Had I told myself that I was afraid, I would have realized that fear was making my decisions irrational. I might have kept relying on my instinctive abilities. Those abilities probably would have seen me through, as they had all morning. Instead I started to convince myself that I had to get Fred back at any cost. But Fred was in worse shape than I and willingly admitted that fact to the court later on. The situation hadn't changed: I had. The obsession was turning to fear. I reached for the reins and said "Whoa."

The morning's events brought me to the realization that the game of Cops and Robbers is complex; all the rules and all the decisions are made by lawyers. It was becoming obvious, even to an egotist, that a layman should be represented by a lawyer with an independent attitude if he wants a reasonable chance of receiving a fair hearing in court, and I had begun the morning with just that lawyer, Fred. When he was taken from me, I had John, who could have handled things even though technically he represented Ginger. I had the constitutional right to serve as my own attorney and by doing so could have used John as a stand-in attorney until I was able to make other arrangements.

Despite my constitutional rights, the Kid had the power to remove Fred by saying that he intended to arrest Fred, without offering any evidence, without providing a signed warrant, without stating the charges.

I looked at my watch. It was 11:40 a.m. I certainly didn't sleep long. As I entered the courtroom I told myself to become more submissive to this system of justice and quit acting like a loose cannon. It was apparent that they would be satisfied if I would just act like any normal human being, whatever that means under these circumstances, and plead guilty. They were so used to barking and growling and snapping and biting as a substitute for doing the work to accomplish their job, that they were having an enormous amount of trouble accepting a large boot to the ass. They were doing whatever they had to do, legal or illegal, to impose their will. I was really having a difficult time adjusting to their thinking.

I asked myself, "How do I act normally?" I had tried in the past and would always fail miserably. The more normal I thought I was acting, the more conspicuous I thought I looked to everyone around me, and I was probably right. I remembered reading in the dictionary words like typical, ordinary, average growth, intelligence, standard, and so on. Frustrated with trying to be normal under Mr. Webster's definitions, I settled on becoming enthusiastic. I don't mean the enthusiasm of the religious zealot or the terrorist with a cause, but enthusiasm for what is important to the people around me; a daughter's blossoming love affair; a new idea for a painting that Ginger is sketching; my grandson's or granddaughter's little league game. Enthusiastic, from the Greek, originally meant "Filled with God." Now that certainly doesn't mean I ever felt my life was filled with God, but I knew that when I was enthusiastically concerned with these truly important issues of my life, I found within me a closer contact with my God. I definitely did not get that feeling playing Cops and Robbers. Looking around at the other players, I got the distinct impression they didn't either.

I walked into the courtroom just as Fred, John, and the Kid emerged from the judge's chambers. Fred had regained a great deal of his composure, but I could tell he was feeling the effects of this morning's blockbuster news. He told me the judge was totally ignoring the fact that I had been appointed my own attorney. He would not even discuss the issue. In addition, the judge had recognized the fact that Fred had been dismissed as my attorney. Therefore, even though I was facing a prison sentence of more than eleven years, he was continuing the hearings leaving me unrepresented.

As difficult as things were for Fred at the time, I could tell he was appalled at the judge's total disregard of the law. Although Fred was always a smart enough attorney to understand the practical aspects of practicing law, he had that wonderful attribute of becoming horrified when judges would make a mockery of their lofty position. I had always wished I could become appalled at something some day, anything, just as Fred does. With Fred, becoming appalled was such an honest emotion, filled with total disdain for the party who totally ignores their responsibility toward society. My fate in life, though, was that there was never anything anyone ever did that I can really remember that horrified or appalled me. I had known Fred for more than eight years. During that time he had always been a sole practitioner. Years earlier he had been a partner of Mel Belli, San Francisco's king of torts. Knowing both men, I found it hard to believe that they were able even to converse with each other, much less be partners. Mel is loud and gregarious, wears expensive suits, and has an opinion on everything. Fred is soft-spoken, a conservative dresser, and an excellent listener. There had been a falling out, and Fred and another attorney left the Belli office to establish a practice more suited to their own personalities. Fred's partner subsequently died, and Fred continued to practice alone.

I always felt comfortable with him even though our personalities were worlds apart. I believed his values were such that no matter what the situation, he would handle it with care and honesty. By contrast, I had done in the past several things of which I was very much ashamed. I had taken out of deals money that I was not entitled to, and I almost always treated my partners with total indifference. In my effort to eliminate that kind of behavior in my life over the past few years, I had been using Fred as a sounding board for right and wrong. At first, I did not have much of a grasp of the right-wrong concept. I worked in a very competitive world, which I found stimulating, and I had no illusions about what it took to compete and succeed. I was still very aggressive so this new experiment in life put me in many crazy and absurd situations. None the least of which I had been facing over the past few months.

The new judge walked onto the bench and we all were required to rise. I was tempted to remain seated and be cited for contempt of court. Had I been so charged, the court would have been absolutely right. I had nothing but contempt for these proceedings and for these judges who let the Kid intimidate Fred with arrest. I stood up, anyway.

The judge was a small man, in his early forties, pompous and not very learned, as judges go. He probably required some political backing somewhere along the line to be sitting on the bench. Over the nine weeks that we were in his court my opinion of him didn't change much. He didn't care a great deal for me, either. I made a point of disrupting the proceedings whenever possible. I believe a court must be respectable to gain respect. Over the weeks, he continued to allow the shadow of Fred's guilt to remain in his courtroom even though Fred was above suspicion. Every time I listened to that judge's lofty pronouncements about the law, I wanted to puke.

When I said "whoa" to myself out in the hall, I committed myself to keeping my mouth shut no matter what happened in hopes they would restore Fred as my attorney. It turned out to be a greater commitment than I had anticipated, in light of what was said in the next few minutes. The judge began by discussing the fact that there seemed to be some confusion as to who represented me. He totally ignored the fact that I already represented myself. He began to explore the possibility of Fred's suitability to serve even though the threat of arrest was hanging over his head. Downstairs, there was no question in anyone's mind that Fred was unable to represent me, as he would have a major conflict of interest. Now, since it had become apparent that without Fred they would have to live with me, Fred's conflict of interest did not loom as menacing, so he became the leading candidate for the attorney of the hour. This hour, at least.

When asked whether he would be able to continue as my attorney, Fred was candid and explained that he was still shaky. He pointed out he would have to find an attorney to represent himself, which was something I had never considered. I couldn't help thinking how funny it was that my attorney would probably have an attorney before I had an attorney since I couldn't be my own attorney and was unable to use Ginger's attorney. The game of Cops and Robbers is simple once you have the hang of it.

All of that made very good sense in light of what we were about to hear next from the Trench-Coat Kid. The judge decided to inquire just why, now, six months after the original arrests and the hearings were about to begin, the Kid had decided to arrest Fred. The Kid stood up, his face flush but his voice unwavering and announced in as deep a voice as his somewhat undersized vocal cords could muster, "Your Honor, we have regarded Mr. Cone to be a suspect since we first began our investigation. Quite obviously, we were very hesitant to pursue this issue without absolute surety of Mr. Cone's guilt since he was the counsel for the defendant. We made a motion to have Mr. Cone removed because we did suspect him, but that motion was denied.

I went into my office yesterday, a Sunday afternoon, to put the final touches on my preparation for today's hearings. While sitting there, all alone, looking at the great number of documents involved in this case, it all came together in my mind and I was convinced of Mr. Costanzo's attorneys implication. There is nothing more I can say, because that is what happened." The judge nodded knowingly as if that sort of thing happened every day and continued with some other part of the proceeding. I wasn't listening to what was going on. I just sat there, mouth open, my chin dropping down to my chest. I was flabbergasted! The Trench-Coat Kid had just stated that Fred had been a suspect for a long time but the Kid did not have any evidence to prove it. Yesterday, in a room all by himself, one day before a hearing that could very well embarrass him and the whole District Attorney's office, he was visited by this intuitive spirit and was now in a position to arrest my defense attorney and have him removed from the case. He gave no reason or evidence to back up his mystical vision, but I'm sure that he appreciated the vision's timely appearance. I could understand what the Kid was doing-he was stalling for time so he could salvage a difficult situation brought on by sheer incompetence. The judge, on the other hand, sat listening to this gobbledygook and did nothing. Just as it was his duty to remove Fred if he had a conflict of interest, it also was his duty to protect Fred from being harassed while performing his obligations to his client. I guess all political systems have people like the judge as well as people like the Fox. I became angrier than I care to admit for just a moment, then caught myself and began to feel better than I had all day. The best I could accomplish with anger would be to create some high drama over how badly Fred, Ginger, and I were being treated. But, as I've always known, I do not become appalled at anyone's actions. When I lie and convince myself that I do, the situation becomes a movie melo- drama. But this courtroom was not Notre Dame, and I was not playing Quasimodo to Ginger's Esmeralda; I was not about to swing down from the bell towers and rescue her and Fred from the gallows-unless, of course, I pled guilty right then, which I had no intention of doing.

Pleading guilty was the only rule in this game that remained constant, so if I decided not to play by that rule my adversaries would continue bending any existing rules until someone caved in from sheer exhaus- tion. Sitting there, I was pretty sure that in the end, that someone would probably be me. But for right now, the game of Cops and Robbers was out of control and so was my taste for it. I enjoyed watching them squirm. I smiled to myself and held back an urge to walk over to the Trench-Coat Kid, give him a great big hug, and tell him to keep hanging in there, baby.

The Kid continued to make excuses for not producing a warrant or even an affidavit of the charges against Fred and received the proper sympathy from the judge. It was decided to break for lunch, with the Kid promising that he would produce some document regarding Fred's alleged arrest for the court to review after the break. You could see the relief on his face as he hurriedly left the courtroom to see what could be drafted in the next two hours. It was obvious to me, if not to everyone present, that he had no evidence whatever to connect Fred with any criminal wrongdoing. I tried to congratulate myself on how well I had beaten them at their own game that morning but I knew that wasn't true. All I had really succeeded in doing was to force them to find some theory to tie Fred into the case, as they had done to Ginger, and actually charge him.

When the court convened again that afternoon, the Kid still came up empty. Although he was unable to give anyone even a hint of what Fred's offenses were, he no longer seemed under any strain. He promised that if the judge would be a nice guy and hold off the proceedings until tomorrow afternoon, he would be able to clear up the log jam in his office and be ready with the infamous signed warrant for Fred's arrest. John argued that his client, Ginger, had the constitutional right to an immediate hearing. She was here and ready to go forward. It made no difference legally to her case if Fred was or was not arrested. Had I been represented by an attorney or even by myself I would have said the same thing. I had the right to move forward as my own attorney there and then, no matter what they decided to do about Fred. Instead, since in the eyes of the court I wasn't represented, I could only sit there and watch myself come closer to serving time in prison. That seemed to be a very convenient set of circumstances for the Kid. Even if it was totally illegal.

The whole matter was put over until the next day at 1:30 p.m. Our right to an immediate hearing was negated, but what concerned me most was what Fred's state of mind would be tomorrow afternoon after sitting around waiting to be arrested. The Kid's new, relaxed demeanor and my instincts combined to tell me that they had decided over the lunch break to begin sweating Fred, to stall as long as they could while Fred became crazy waiting for the axe to fall. If that was the situation, they would not have the warrant ready tomorrow, either. Well, there wasn't anything I could do about that now. Best to keep it to myself. I'll know tomorrow at 1:30 p.m. We all left the courtroom a little washed out. I didn't even care if they took the matter of a speedy hearing to the Supreme Court. Actually, I just waited until a few days later to discuss it with Fred, much to his dismay. No matter what the Kid looked like, I had the feeling that he felt about as washed out as we did. Even if he sweated Fred for a few days, he still had his work cut out. Sooner or later he would have to produce the warrant, so he would now have to begin digging through the forty boxes of files that they had confiscated on the day of the arrest to find something, anything, that he could charge Fred with. I knew what was in those boxes, and I also knew exactly how Fred involved himself in the business. He was clean as a whistle.

Back at John's office, we all agreed that we were all too tired to do much else and should meet tomorrow. Besides, Fred had to go find an attorney for himself. I told him to get one for me if the chance presented itself. I wasn't very hopeful. We walked across the street to the car and I asked Ginger to drive. In the car I closed my eyes and thought of home, that place we left so long ago this morning. My home life was really showing the strain of this ugly game. Cops and Robbers is ugly, but I knew that wasn't what was bothering me. It was my obsession to play. I needed a conscious contact with that Spiritual Being that I have always called God, but right at this moment I knew whatever little contact I did have was quickly slipping away. I knew the obsession was taking over and those moments of real peace were leaving. Peace? What's that about? My God, it occurred to me that I wasn't even able to completely enjoy this year's Easter party.

# CHAPTER 7

# The Easter Party

Home, Easter Morning, April 1984: My first thought that morning was not about the arrests: it was to realize that today was Easter Sunday. The arrests were my second thought. That was an improvement over all the previous mornings since the day they scooped Ginger and me off the street and into jail. Those stupid arrests had become my first thought in the morning, my last thought at night, and most of the thoughts in between. I couldn't believe how obsessive I had become about them. It was becoming apparent that those thought processes were just like the thought processes I had when I was using alcohol, they consumed my mind completely. I had become totally caught up in them. I needed to work on my attitude.

I tried to recall my last thought last night and started to delude myself that it was about the Easter Party. Then I said to myself, "Come on, get real," and I remembered how I was going over a section Fred told me about in the criminal code that would let me file criminal charges against the Kid for not allowing Fred to be with me at the house on the morning of the arrest. I thought I'd love to file those charges and watch the Kid squirm. I got hold of myself and realized I had to stop thinking like that. This wasn't a game; Ginger was on the hook, too. It was terrible having her in the middle of this fight. It left me at such a disadvantage. I thought I could understand how it feels to have a member of your family kidnaped. You have to consider the consequences of every action. I felt I needed to be that careful. Had Ginger not been involved, I would have filed the charges against the Kid in a hot second and probably break that story about the Fox and his flaky relatives, as well.

What was I thinking about? I knew I really must stop that kind of thinking. It wasn't healthy for me and it certainly did not create a healthy climate for the family. It was an absolute necessity to quit planning and scheming so I could pay adequate attention to the other, more important parts of my life-Ginger, the family, and business. I was going to enjoy myself today. It would be a wonderful Easter party. It was essential not to destroy the day, to keep in the forefront of my mind that my happiness depends on whether I decide to be happy, not on what other people do or say. I knew I should resume meditating for five minutes each morning. I learned to do it early on in my twelve step program, and it never failed to take away the compulsions in my life. It was such a pain to start again.

The paper hadn't been delivered yet. It was only five-thirty in the morning. I looked at Ginger, still sound asleep, even though the fool whom she decided, for whatever reason, to spend her life with, had just turned on the lights in the bedroom and was rustling around creating enough noise to wake the dead. It was too bad the paper wasn't there, though, so I could go back to bed, have a cup of coffee and read the comics, especially Prince Valiant. I knew that by the time the paper arrived I would be too busy to read it so I would probably miss Prince Valiant today. My week always starts off lousy when I miss reading him. I wondered whether they let you have the paper in prison. It would be awful to go a long time without my weekly dose of the Prince and all his Camelot buddies. I caught myself and thought, "Will you stop that nonsense about prison?"

The coffee was already made. Either Dorothy, the housekeeper...I stopped abruptly to remind myself to quit referring to Dorothy as a housekeeper. She was our friend. I wondered how I got in the habit of referring to her as a housekeeper? After all, she took care of my home,

Damon, my youngest son, and the grandchildren. Responsibilities of that nature are never left to a housekeeper. The obsession of the arrests had dulled my best instincts. I honestly cared for Dorothy and knew the importance of showing her the respect she deserved. Whatever I called her, God bless her, because I sure needed a cup of coffee right then. I poured another cup and decided to walk around the yard to check on things for the party. Ginger had told me that our daughter, our son-in-law, and the grandchildren would not be there for the party. They had informed her that since I had accused him of something he denies doing, they no longer wanted to have anything to do with the family. "Good Lord," I said to myself, "What a sad state of affairs." I had handled it all so badly. I wondered why I had said anything about it in the first place. I was sure he was the informant, but after the initial anger it no longer seemed important. Well, not too important.

For the first time I questioned whether playing the game of Cops and Robbers was worth all the destruction and havoc that was raining down on my family. Dorothy had told me that our daughters had words the other day. I was amazed. My daughters had always been so close. I promised myself that when I saw my son-in-law again I would apologize. That ought to be an interesting conversation, because I was sure he would never believe that my family meant more to me than being mad at him. I said to myself, "Yeah, that's a good idea. When I see him next, I'll apologize to the son-of-a-bitch." I was prepared to make concessions, but it would be a long time before the milk of human kindness would flow through my veins when it came to the subject of my son-in-law. I was sure John could make a deal for me to plead guilty. That deal would include letting Ginger go free and sentencing me to only a year or so. It was curious why I found saying that I'm guilty in a courtroom so difficult. I'm sure the words would stick in my throat.

What possible difference would it make if I plea bargained? In my heart I was convinced they would probably convict me sooner or later. I was, in effect lying to Ginger by not telling her that I thought I could make a deal. There is no way to reconcile lying with the love I feel for her. I knew the trouble: I was afraid her practical side would tell me to plead guilty and be done with the whole sordid affair once and for all. It would be only fair to Ginger for me to plead guilty no matter what I think personally and get her out of danger. Then I could let those Shylocks extract their pound of flesh. I was pretty sure that going to jail would not scare me. Actually it would be a relief from these constant battles in court. "So why not do it? Do it now!" I told myself. This dilemma had been tearing me apart for too long. "God, I just can't seem to roll over and quit! They are blackmailing me by arresting Ginger! I hate it, but I am driven to keep fighting" I recognized that I had lost all conscious contact with that wonderful Higher Spirit, my own personal God who found me dying in that little room and restored all the beauty in my life. I had always turned to that Spirit to make all my major decisions: now I kept holding on to my own self-will and I knew that false pride, obsession, or whatever it was would destroy all the beauty again. I was becoming almost hysterical.

I decided to go down by the river and pull myself together. It was so peaceful and serene by the river. A slight wind was blowing through the trees, and the river was still high from the winter thaws. I skipped a few rocks over the water as it flowed gracefully toward the Pacific Ocean. All I wanted from life was peace. No, I knew that wasn't the truth. I didn't care about having peace. The truth was that I wanted to continue fighting and yet be completely honest with Ginger and the kids. My self-will was rapidly becoming hard to control, running rampant over everyone. After settling down, getting hold of my emotions, trying to find God in this wonderful quiet place; the simple act of sitting there alone for a few minutes made me realize that I couldn't go any further. I needed to tell Ginger that I thought I could make a deal, even though I really wanted to cram any deal offered by the Kid up his nose. I became very conscious of the fact that I desperately wanted to continue fighting, but a familiar little voice inside me, the one that had seen me through so many crises in the past and the one I had lately chosen to ignore, told me to tell the truth and take my chances. I went with the voice and made the decision to become rigorously honest with the woman I loved so much. The realization that I was about to tell Ginger the truth caused the noise in my head, all those thoughts that were driving me crazy, to cease and I became tranquil. I thought, "I'll tell her but we don't have to make that decision today; we'll have a great Easter party, sharing our love and our life with our children, friends and relatives. No one should celebrate with a lie in his heart."

I drove back to the house, woke Ginger, and blurted it out.

She sat up in bed rubbing the sleep out of her eyes, giving me the same sigh that Fred gives me when I tell him how we should set up camp at the Supreme Court on all the important legal issues I bring to him, and she said, "Honey, you mean to tell me you woke me up to tell me that? John said something to me about two weeks ago and I never thought to mention it. I figured we could cross that bridge when we come to it. Now, for heaven's sake, get out of here and let me go back to sleep."

Our spectacular Easter parties were conceived harmlessly enough. Almost twenty years before, when all our children were young, I was working in Orange County, in Southern California, for a company that completed and sold condominium and housing projects in which the original builder, having serious financial problems, had abandoned the project, leaving it partially completed. This company was doing much the same thing as my company was doing when they arrested me. It was our job to clean up the mess the builder had left. Ginger and I lived in a beautiful company house with our four children. My cousin Ella and her husband also worked for the company and lived in the house next door with their four children, about the same age as ours. We spent a couple of years living as one big happy family. Each child usually brought home a friend or two, so if all of the little lights of my life-children, nephews, nieces, and their compadres-were stationed at our house for more than 15 minutes the noise level easily exceeded that of the jail tank. In addition, no matter how well stocked Ginger left the refrigerator, all food, drink, and especially sweets would quickly disappear. On Sunday mornings we all gathered next door to delight in Ella's husband's "world-famous" pancakes. I made ramos fizzes while he prepared the pancake batter, so it is difficult to remember whether the pancakes were actually world-famous because by the time I sat down I was usually sloshed. So was anyone else who didn't have the good sense not to drink my concoction, because I purposely made them much too strong; but the sweet milkshake-like drink disguised the flavor of the alcohol.

It was in that atmosphere one Sunday that we were all trying to decide how we should celebrate the upcoming Easter. I reminisced how as a boy our grandfather would buy a goat. I couldn't remember ever having actually eaten the goat, but I distinctly remember him bringing it home before Easter. We all decided that we should celebrate Easter in the genuine, old-country Italian way, inviting what eventually seemed like everyone in the world to our party-and cook a goat. Ella and Ginger were assigned to find a goat. After running into a brick wall at all the meat markets in the area, they decided to go to an auction and buy one on the hoof. Every farmer in Orange County watched and snickered as these two young girls, dressed in clothes designed more for Beverly Hills than for an animal auction, tried to make bids. They were finally successful, but upon closer examination, after the purchase, they discovered they had acquired a pregnant nanny. The farmers all had a great laugh, but eventually took pity on them and allowed them to return the nanny and get a kid goat, which turned out to be the first of many we cooked to celebrate Easter as an Italian holiday. Such parties became an annual even, and although the format was changed through the years, there was always a goat and a huge Easter egg hunt for the children. Normally, we hired someone in an Easter Bunny costume to mystify the children and supervise the hunt.The child finding the golden egg got a special Easter basket containing a enormous chocolate Easter Bunny. As time went on we had, at the various parties, clowns, accordion players. Once we even had a greased pig race.

I put the goat on the spit early in the morning so I wouldn't miss the Easter egg hunt. Many people had arrived the day before; some were awake, and there was a great deal of hustle and bustle in the house when I returned from the meditation at the river. Children of every size, shape, and sex were running around trying to be the first to show me the basket the Easter Bunny had brought them. Dorothy had started breakfast and some people scurried to make the eight o'clock mass.

My father-in-law, Charlie, who over the years had become my dear friend, was up early, as usual, and had walked his dog, or vice-versa. While standing at the spit waiting for the coals to become hot, I repeated to him the story of our first cup of coffee together, which always made him chuckle: A few months before Ginger and I were married, she had taken a job in Grass Valley and had rented a small apartment there. I was working the swing shift in San Francisco at the Federal Reserve Bank, had just been paid, and it was Friday, the evening before a three-day weekend. After work, about 1:00 a.m., I hopped in my car and roared toward Grass Valley. Upon arriving at Ginger's apartment I decided to surprise her and go around back and crawl through the bedroom window instead of using the standard means of entry, the front door. Mrs. Costanzo's son was not too bright on his best day, much less when he was madly in love. The window opened quietly (I had tried it before), I slipped through, tiptoed across the room to the sleeping beauty under the covers, and whispered, "Hi, Honey, It's me." The sleeping beauty-or the body I thought was the sleeping beauty-rolled over and said, in a voice that was definitely not the tender, responsive voice I had anticipated, "What are you doing here at this time of night?" Good Heavens! It was Ginger's father and his mood was not good.

My first impulse was to run, but I was in such shock my body refused to move. All I could think to say was, "Hi, Mr. Johnson, how are you this morning?" He was more than likely in some sort of shock, too; he just sat on the bed staring at me for what felt like eternity, trying to determine what to do with this idiotic-looking kid who showed up in his daughter's bedroom in the middle of the night. I thought he was about to hit me over the head with the lamp, but he just sighed and said in his quiet and soft spoken way, "Ginger's visiting her girlfriend. You must be tired after the long drive. Let's go into the kitchen and I'll fix some coffee."

I sat quietly at the kitchen table, trying to look like a repentant sinner making amends for all my past indiscretions. He continued to go about the business of the coffee and finally remarked that he wasn't sure how to use Ginger's coffee maker, so he put some grounds on the bottom of the pan and poured hot water over them, poured me a cup, and said he would have some later.

"Go ahead, drink up," he said sounding as though that was not a suggestion but an order, and I found myself drinking hot water filled with coffee grounds, with a great big mock grin on my face. I detected that Charlie was sporting a wry smile, but I drank my medicine and politely refused a second cup. Our relationship had changed over the years. (There we were sitting in the manicured yard of my beautiful home with it's magnificent swimming pool.) He had spent every holiday with us for over thirty years. He had retired in a house that he and I had purchased together many years ago as a vacation retreat in Grass Valley. We both had been heavy drinkers and had some pretty wild times, but neither of us drank anymore. We laughed about some of the things we did, though.

I enjoyed laughing with Charlie. This was the man my son had gone to after the arrests to help raise bail. After my son's phone call, this eighty-five-year-old man had gone to his safety deposit box and took out all his securities, savings passbooks, bonds, and other paper of value, and put them on the kitchen table. The amount was considerable. When my son, Frank, arrived his grandfather told him to take whatever he needed. That story truly touched me.

He chuckled again when he heard the story about the coffee as he always does, but-even after more than thirty years-made no attempt to confess his guilt. I guess no one was in the mood to plead guilty that day.

The party was, without a doubt, the most successful one we had ever had. The goat turned out terrible, but it was only symbolic, anyway. The food that we provided coupled with the food others brought could have fed twice the number of party goers. There was so much spaghetti we served it in washtubs, as we did the salads. Chicken and meatballs, great pots of beans simmered on the stove, hors d'oeuvres, dips, chips, peanuts, and other comestibles were everywhere. Casseroles and vegetables were lined up on the table. That's what an Italian party is all about.

The morning had been overcast, but the sun came out and the children jumped in the pool while the music played and the grownups, from seventeen to eighty-five, danced. The Easter Bunny showed up on time and someone found the golden egg and was awarded the basket with the big chocolate bunny. Everyone received a personal homemade basket, the handiwork of someone else at the party, a basket filled with love from a loved one. I have always enjoyed the sense of family and tradition. It is a gift given to very few in today's world, and one of my dearest wishes is that my children pass it along.

That evening I went to bed thoroughly happy and contented with the world, physically exhausted and telling myself I would sleep in. I closed my eyes thinking God had returned to my life and nothing could harm me now. Just as I began to close my eyes I wondered whether I should really file those charges against the Kid? Cops and Robbers consumed me and its noise returned in my head. I was addicted once again. My stomach muscles tightened. I felt awful. The game owned my life.

# CHAPTER 8

# The Anger

We returned to the courtroom at 1:30 p.m. Tuesday afternoon, the time the judge had decided the Kid had to produce some tangible evidence on when, how, and why he intended to arrest Fred. Much to everyone's surprise, (except mine), the Kid had absolutely nothing to produce. Not only could he not produce the warrant for Fred's arrest, he still refused to give the judge any details of what crime Fred had committed or when that elusive information would be available. I had already stated that I wanted to be represented by Fred and that the hearings should get under way immediately. Either he was under arrest or he was not. It certainly seemed simple enough. If he was not under arrest, as was obvious to all persons present, and no one had any specific information as to how and why he would be arrested, then he should have the right to represent me without any interference. That is the letter of the law; it is the spirit of the law. To be represented by the attorney of one's choice is a fundamental right given each citizen in the Sixth amendment of the Constitution.

The judge began to hedge, and at that moment he lost all credibility he would ever have posing as a judge. He ruled that the hearings should proceed, with the condition that Fred could serve only as my temporary attorney until the District Attorney's office decided whether they could find enough-or for that matter, any-evidence to justify arresting him.

For the second day in a row I felt like a one-legged man in a sack race. Fred had become a wreck.

The day before, he had gone to see a couple of old friends in town who practiced law and was politely but firmly refused personal representation. Apparently, the word had gotten out that he was now persona non grata in the legal community. I think he was more hurt than scared. He looked to be very ragged. To watch his old colleagues abandon him in an hour of crisis was a terrible shock. I felt a great deal of compassion. He was such a kind, veracious, sensitive human being. He deserved better from a profession he had served so well for so long. So we entered the courtroom that afternoon with neither Fred nor I represented by legal counsel.

When Fred and I met at his hotel early that morning before court and took a long walk together, the focus of our conversation was his arrest rather than what we would face in court that day. That was totally unlike him. He appeared to be functioning at a reasonable level once we were inside the courtroom, but it was obvious that he had gotten very little sleep. I wasn't sure how many more days he could hang in.

The game of Cops and Robbers was certainly a fascinating game to play. Only the best of players would survive the first few hands if, as appeared to be happening, the opposing side continued running this game until the wheels fell off. I was pretty sure that was how the opposing team had decided to proceed after they had reviewed yesterday's events. On the other hand, I was finding myself becoming more apprehensive about continuing to play that way. After all, when all the chips were on the table, our team had the most to lose.

I had done a bit of reviewing myself. It was obvious that this judge would never let me represent myself. That was made clear to me yesterday. Finding someone else would be economically impossible. I had already paid most of Fred and John's fees and could not raise enough cash for a new attorney's retainer on such short notice. It was a pretty good bet, judging from the response Fred received from the local bar establishment, that they wouldn't want to represent me at any price. Bringing someone from San Francisco would be the only possibility but the attorney would have to abandon his practice for a case out of town, where the local authorities were threatening to arrest the attorney he was replacing. In trying to analyze the whole thing, I wasn't sure that I could even retain someone from San Francisco.

So I had to try to keep Fred no matter what the circumstances, and I could only believe those circumstances would become worse. With me having no attorney whatsoever, the Kid's options become limitless. A chilling thought crossed my mind. Suppose during the interim period, while I am looking for an attorney, the Kid made a motion to increase my bail substantially. From what I've witnessed over the past couple of days, there was no question in my mind that this judge would grant it. I would then be forced to lounge around a jail cell for a few days while more bail was posted. It would substantially reduce my available cash and effectively close these current hearings, posthaste.

It became clear that I personally didn't have a snowball's chance in Hell of winning anything out of these hearings. The die was cast. It was quite difficult to admit that I had already lost even before the hearings began, but I tried to accept that fact so I would be able to concentrate my attention on a more constructive course of action. Once I had accepted that I would lose, the obvious next step was to make sure Ginger was acquitted. I had a plan!

I listened to the advice John gave Ginger about her courtroom demeanor several days before the hearings were scheduled to begin. He told her to dress very conservatively, to keep her hands folded whenever she could, and definitely to not take notes during the hearings or appear efficient in any way. I took this all in with a great deal of fascination only because we were going before a judge and not a jury. I could understand that it would be important to gain every possible advantage so as not to prejudice a jury, but certainly a judge had more sense then to think that just because someone is prudent enough to take notes at a hearing involving loss of their freedom, it would not necessarily mean that she would be involved in some grand conspiracy to defraud. After watching and listening to this man sitting behind that imposing bench yesterday and today, there was no question in my mind that would be exactly what he would think.

I determined that if, in fact, he could be swayed more by what he saw rather than by the testimony he would hear, I would let him see exactly what he had already made up his mind he was going to see. If I was correct in my assessment that I had no chance whatsoever of helping my own cause in the upcoming hearings, then I might as well create a diversion to help Ginger's cause. It took very little effort for me to act like the biggest, and most obnoxious jerk the world has ever seen. I have had some practice. I decided to use those God-given talents in this courtroom, and let the judge see how this poor, sweet, woman is completely bullied by this awful man, before whom she cowered at the slightest change in his voice level. I hoped to create enough sympathy for Ginger to transcend any judgments he already harbored against her.

Even though I was apprehensive, my obsession with the game of Cops and Robbers was stronger; I decided to show my contempt for the whole farce-not by disrupting the proceedings; all that would get me was a contempt of court charge. My plan was to use facial expressions, slouch in my chair, and moan during some of the Fox's more obvious lies. When I spoke to either Fred or John I would refer to the Kid and the Fox as Herkimer and Jerkimer, in a voice just loud enough for the judge to hear without giving the impression I had intended him to hear. I knew both attorneys would castigate me-but that would only enhance my image of contempt. I envisioned Fred heaving great sighs, and if he did I would tone down my game for a while, if for no other reason than to relieve my friend's burden of having me for a client. The first afternoon of the hearings went pretty much as expected. My son-in-law was called to the stand and freely admitted, much to the chagrin of the Kid, that he acted as a confidential informant for law enforcement. He testified that he did so without my daughter's knowledge. He said that he told my daughter, with the consent of the Kid, that she was to be arrested, but the Kid could get her immunity from prosecution if she testified against her parents. To her credit, she asked our permission before she accepted the offer, and we readily gave it. It turned out that my son-in-law insisted on acting as her attorney throughout her testimony, and she certainly did not receive the independent advice she deserved.

Our daughter was eight and one-half months pregnant at the time, but the Kid demanded she give the testimony immediately, ignoring her very delicate state rather than waiting thirty days until she had the baby and was better able to deal with an ordeal of that magnitude. My son-in-law readily testified that he had lied to the law enforcement officials he had met with on several occasions, but became very vague in replying to the questions about a personal immunity deal. My son-in-law's testimony was disgusting. Frankly, I was sorry we called him as a witness, because even though I believed he was the informer, I had an element of doubt. I should have realized that the doubt was infinitely preferable to the truth I was forced to hear that afternoon.

On Wednesday morning the Kid again showed up without a warrant or an explanation as to why they intended to arrest Fred. He wasn't even embarrassed. The judge continued to shrug; continuing to decline to protect Fred against all the harassment. I knew I had been right on Monday when I guessed they would try to sweat Fred. That strategy was taking its toll on him. Being arrested is immeasurably better than standing around waiting for it to happen. It's always easier to deal with the devil you know than with the devil you don't know.

I wish now I had just pled guilty and eliminated Fred's suffering. The game of Cops and Robbers had robbed me of my honor, just as alcohol had so many years ago. Fred was my friend. Both Ginger and he should have come first in all my decisions. I should have been willing to ride the beef no matter what my feelings were of guilt or innocence. I did, anyway, because it was my beef to ride. I was the one-not Fred, not

Ginger-who had made all major decisions in the company. I should have accepted the consequences. I was asking too much of Fred. My inability to turn myself in and free the hostages, no matter how disagreeable it seemed, in this saga of misguided justice and ethics on both sides was, without question, the lowest point of my life. My hope is that as the events unfolded, my actions restored at least a portion of my lost honor.

By Thursday when the Kid walked into the courtroom and announced once again that he did not have a warrant and gave no reason why he planned to arrest Fred, I lost my patience. I was fed up with his games. My face became flush, my palms were sweating, and I was very angry with a frightening kind of anger I had not felt in a long time. Suddenly, I was on my feet demanding-in a loud voice-that Fred put a stop to this charade. I was screaming for him to stand in the middle of the courtroom and give the Kid the finger, then tell his hokey judge to do the job he was hired to do, to take charge of his own courtroom rather than remain a marionette for the District Attorney's office.

Fred grabbed my arm and tried to pull me down, but I pushed him away. I guess my voice had started to reverberate off the walls, because even the judge and the bailiff were taken by surprise. The bailiff was rushing toward me with his gun out. I was so upset that I could not distinguish the faces around me, just images; Fred, John, the bailiff. Somehow a quick recess was called and they rushed me out into the corridor to try to settle me down before I could poke Herkimer and Jerkimer in the nose and do the same for any companions that they could find under that rock they had crawled out from under.

It occurred to me when I calmed down somewhat after getting a soothing hug from Ginger, walking up and down the hallway, and talking to Fred and John for a while, that I could be under more strain than I had noticed. My John Wayne image was wearing thin and I was becoming afraid of this game of Cops and Robbers. Playing the game without a legitimate attorney to represent me was draining my energy.

At the beginning of the week I felt self-assured and was building a little confidence that we might even have a chance to win. By now it was becoming obvious to me that without an independent attorney of Fred's caliber I would be lucky to save Ginger.

What bothered me most was that I seemed to be reverting to that uncontrollable, frustrated, angry young man I had been so long ago: the young man who drank gallons of alcohol and masked his all-consuming fears by intimidating others; the young man who used to stuff feelings of love deep inside him to protect them from a world he was convinced would reject them; the young man who replaced honesty-even loud, obnoxious honesty-with scheming because it was imperative always to completely control the events surrounding him; the young man who never dealt with his plague, supposedly cured years before, of constantly blaming others for his own failings.

I let those thoughts bother me for only a while, then rejected them, consciously, so I would become able once again to resume the game of Cops and Robbers. In dismissing these considerations, I denied their existence. A little voice in the back of my brain, which had been quiet for many years, told me, "After all, nobody's perfect. Especially men like you who are tough, real tough." I should have recognized that voice immediately-it was the one that always told me things were fine even when I was hearing the rustling of leaves. There may still have been time in all of this to find shelter, but I was fascinated by the storm. What is truly amazing is that I continued to carry on the fascination for the game even though I was aware that my family, my friends, and I were about to be blown away. Reliving those feelings of anger I experienced that day in the courtroom, I'm filled with mixed emotions. The reminders of a well meaning young man whose good intentions even-tually turned to alcohol, fear, anger, and the gates of death. It is difficult to remember my life as a young man without trying to analyze the actions of that well intentioned youth rather than accept it all and try to change and move on.

Whenever I have thoughts of my younger years I always remember my overwhelming desire for achievement in business. The strange places that this desire took me and the legacy of turmoil it left. I do not regret it too much or care to shut the door on it. It is just the truth of my life. I don't particularly see it all as right or wrong because that is how it happened and I do not have the ability to change it now. My real life has always been centered around family, children and love. So when all is said and done, the achievements of my life come from those areas. Money and success gave very little long-term satisfaction and usually left me overwrought and frustrated.

Several months after our marriage we moved to San Francisco from Grass Valley. When our first child, Caren, was born it seemed to me to be a miracle, which I guess it was. I can still remember carrying her down the steps of the hospital, and feeling a glow inside my body I had never felt before. The next day on my way to work I became filled with this excruciating fear of how I would ever support Ginger and the baby. I didn't really understand too much about this new world of wives and babies that had sort of flowed into my life without me even knowing it had taken place. What I knew instinctively, though, was that babies needed a mother around them and I had to find some way to make sure that Ginger would never be required to work so that Caren, and Ginger for that matter, would always be happy and secure in their lives. I decided to enroll in a business college and become a professional.

Actually, I didn't have the slightest idea what a professional was or did. I must have picked the word up in a movie somewhere and gave it my own connotation. Still, if I could become a professional all my worries would be behind me. The college had a wonderful catalog on the classes available to budding professionals like me, and I eagerly studied the requirements demanded for the different professions-surprised to find how much work it would require to reach my goal. What I sort of had in mind was a six month course, taking classes a couple of nights a week. Instead, they talked of requirements that extended into years.

What a drag! "Well," I thought, "Ginger and Caren were worth it, so I might as well get the show on the road. The sooner I start, the sooner I'll finish."

Since I knew nothing about any profession, I was forced to pick one by trying to determine which one would be the easiest: Lawyer, Certified Public Accountant, Advertising, Real Estate, or Traffic Manager. I had never heard of a Certified Public Accountant, so I said to myself, "How tough can it be if no one has ever heard of a CPA." I will admit that at that age I had an enormous amount of love for my little family, but I certainly was not long on mental discipline. My first semester was a nightmare; I worked during the day, went to school four nights a week, and studied on the weekends after working all night Friday and Saturday in a gas station. I was finally able to discern a debit from a credit, stay awake in class, and hand in all my homework on time so I remained in school for the second semester. I had truly become a budding professional. The years passed and we had two more daughters, Julie and Janice. For the life of me, I'll never quite figure out when I found the time or energy. Ain't love grand! At twenty five years old I passed the CPA examination, went into business for myself, and became instantly successful. My energy knew few limitations. I was a fair CPA with an ability to hire excellent CPAs. In a profession that was famous for its conservative thinking and dull people, I had a free spirit with the ability to literally sell snow to the Eskimos! In 1959 we moved to Marin County, an exclusive area north of San Francisco, to a house with a swimming pool. My poor mother, whose idea of luxury was a Maytag washer with a wringer attachment, almost fainted when she first saw the house and the pool. Most of my clients were young builders coming to that area and staking their claim, as I was, to fame and fortune. Drinking became a way of life with us because, after all, look at us, successful, young, energetic. What could force any of us from the crest of the wave. Life for me was hectic but for the most part, sunny and warm. I soon tired of being a professional. Operating a business on a day to day basis did not create for me the excitement so necessary to maintain the limitless energy I required to drive that overwhelming desire to achieve. I sold my firm and became a promoter. I opened offices in New York and San Francisco, becoming a simple peddler of large publicly held companies and large real estate projects, making far more money than my services were worth. That is the nature of that type of business, as is the entertainment and sports business. It was terribly exciting for awhile, but soon took on the same drudgery as the CPA firm. I hated the constant traveling that carries with it the loneliness of being away from the ones you love. Many years ago the group "Chicago" recorded a song written about the loneliness of living on the road, wishing the one they loved was with them. I immediately related to the lyrics. I imagine anyone who travels constantly would too.

My business was flourishing and eventually we moved into a twenty-two room mansion. Whenever I was home I would wake up early, walk down the circular driveway, turn around and see this absolutely spectacular house, comforted that Ginger and all four children (by that time my son Frank had been born), were sleeping contentedly and safe inside. I would always be dead tired, and usually be recovering from a hangover, but I would try to convince myself that it really didn't matter. Those fears I had experienced going to work that day after Caren was born had been overcome. At least, that was what I kept telling myself, ignoring all the while, the sound of rustling leaves on the lawn as I trudged back to the house.

By 1969, just ten years after I had opened my original CPA office, I was totally burnt out; I no longer had the unlimited energy that once was my trademark. In fact, I no longer cared about work and was only going through the motions. The business fell apart. I was angry at everyone for what I thought they were doing to me and solved that problem easily enough by drinking more until everything was gone.

Standing in the courthouse corridor, while trying to calm down, it occurred to me that the old anger had returned.

Before the afternoon session began, the Kid met with Fred and John in the hallway, apart from where Ginger and I were standing. I couldn't hear what they were saying, but I wasn't surprised that a meeting was taking place. I thought the Kid had gotten just about as much mileage as he was going to get by threatening to arrest Fred; the time was drawing near when he would have to put up or shut up. Something had to give, and, thinking back on my performance that morning, I hoped I would hold my temper until something did. The meeting lasted only a few minutes when both attorneys returned with those familiar, somber faces to which I had become accustomed over the past few days. The expressions I had come to recognize as someone's cue to throw a pie in my face. I sure had a lot of pies thrown in my face in the last few days. "Fred, are you kidding me?" I asked when Fred told me the gist of the meeting. "Do you mean the best he can come up with to justify threatening to arrest you is a letter you wrote saying that I sent you a check to resolve a lawsuit and that you deposited that check in your trust account? But he doesn't believe that you actually deposited the check?" I could feel my anger returning despite my resolution to keep it in check. "He has no evidence one way or another to make the accusation, so he's just saying he doesn't believe you. I suppose this all occurred to him last Sunday, while sitting around his office, all alone. A magic voice suddenly told him that you just didn't deposit the check, and he should now arrest you. For Christ's sake, Fred, why the hell doesn't he just call the bank and find out? It wouldn't take more than five minutes!"

I could see Fred's distress. He was obviously fighting a terrible battle with himself, but I was mystified as to what the problem could be. Hell, just call the bank.

"I told him the same thing about the bank," Fred answered, "but he has demanded to see my personal attorney's trust account to verify the deposit was made. He said if I let them see my trust account, and they see that I, in fact, deposited your check, then they won't arrest me." As Fred spoke I guessed he was completely torn between his sense of duty to me and his desire to be free from the threat of arrest.

"Then show him the records of your trust account. Christ, you deposited the check, so what's the big deal?" I suspected those were empty words because this dilemma was much more complicated than it would appear to a layman. I braced myself for Fred's reply.

"Frank, if I show him the records of my trust account on this transaction, that becomes evidence, and he will be able to call me as a prosecution witness at the trial," Fred told me sheepishly.? Ah, the plot thickens," I thought. "Now I have the choice of refusing to have Fred show them his records and face the possibility of his arrest on a total fabrication, or letting him show them the records and have my own attorney testify as a prosecution witness." It seemed to me at the time that it would be difficult not to become a fan of the game of Cops and Robbers. They were playing the game with such inspiration that it was almost an art form. (the odds of my winning were infinitely better playing against the house in any game in Las Vegas.)

Fred and John discussed with me the implications at length. I paid little attention to what they were saying. At that point it made little difference. All that mattered to me was that I was the prime defendant in a major criminal case, and I was going to court each day unrepresented. If I didn't do something quick, my future would be eleven and one-half years in the slammer. Their advice involved something distant and remote, something that meant almost nothing to me. I had never even seen, much less participated in, a jury trial. What was real to me was that I had been sitting in a courtroom for three and one-half days with a man who, by his own admission, was coming apart at the seams over fear of arrest, and who was the only person qualified to represent me without going through a major educational process. I was forced to choose; if I wanted him as my attorney, then I had to agree to his being a witness for the prosecution. Some choice. I agreed reluctantly and was not sure whether I did it to save Fred or to get him back operating on all eight cylinders. I hate to admit that the selfish motive was the dominant factor. That evening the records were brought from Fred's San Francisco office and, of course, they showed he had deposited the check-just as the letter in question stated. A fact of which I was sure the Kid was already aware.

The next day they brought Ginger and me into the judge's chambers and the judge reiterated the implications of our agreement to release the records. The most important item being that Fred could be called as a prosecution witness. He even had the court reporter take down everything that was said, so he had on record that he had performed his duty. He left unsaid that I was being blackmailed. Everyone in the room knew Fred had deposited the check. If he hadn't, why would we have been there in the first place? We were there to hand Fred over as a prosecution witness, not to look at some silly documents. The judge was a sorry excuse for the position he held because he condoned the whole charade.

It required an hour for the judge and each attorney to give a little speech on how Ginger and I had been thoroughly advised of our rights by each of them so the record would reflect the high ethical standards with which this whole matter was being handled. Fred finally turned the records over, and after examining the deposit slip and bank statements, the Kid remarked that he was now satisfied that Fred was innocent. Big news! We all got up to leave and the Kid decided to make one more statement before our little session ended. Looking quite smug, he raised himself to his full five-foot-eight height and casually remarked, "We all agree that Fred did nothing wrong in this instance, but we plan to keep on looking; if we find anything else we will arrest him on the spot."

I no longer had the desire or inclination to become angry. Those feelings had subsided the day before. Of course, I realized that the Kid's statement meant we had accomplished nothing by turning over the records and allowing Fred to become a prosecution witness. They still held the threat of arrest over my defense attorney's head. At any time they could retrieve some innocuous letter from more than forty boxes of files they had confiscated, receive a message from some spirit that dwells only in the offices of the District Attorney, and emerges only at their convenience, contend that the contents of the new letter are false, and start the whole process again.

At that moment I knew there was nothing to the game of Cops and Robbers. It was strictly a game. There was no substance to it other than what was in the minds of these players, and I had yet to meet anyone, except Fred and John, with any intelligence. Whoever these people around me were-the judge, the Kid, and the Fox-I hoped they were not representative of the justice system as a whole. They had no concept of the letter of the law, much less the spirit of the law. They all made me feel dirty. I recalled in that flash their constant intimidation of innocent persons like Ginger, Fred, and my daughter, and the judge's silent agreement to their deeds. My mood became dark. It didn't make much difference to me any more if they slapped me with a contempt of court charge. That court was absolutely contemptible. The obsession now had complete control of me. I turned around, stared directly at the Kid and, much to the amazement of everyone in the room, gave him the finger and said, "Fuck you, Kid," and walked out.

# CHAPTER 9

# Folsom Reflections

*Folsom Prison, March 1986:* I'm becoming tired of sitting in this cell beating the dead dog of the courtrooms. I'd prefer spending a little time describing the society within a society which now I call my domicile.

My cellmate made beans last night in a little pot that looks like a small percolator and plugs into the wall socket. They were so hot I could barely swallow them and my eyes watered continuously, but they were so delicious I couldn't stop eating them. We both began to sweat so much we had to strip down to our shorts, even though it is still winter. He promised to make them once a week. My God, if they keep me here any length of time the beans will eat the walls of my stomach.

The food they serve in this place will never receive a four-star rating on the best restaurant list. I'm sure it is one of the reasons my travel agent rates the tour so poorly. The menu can be described with one word: grease. To their credit, they do provide certain staples that, if self-discipline is used, provide an adequate and healthful diet.

For breakfast I eat either dry cereal or oatmeal with milk and fruit, or fruit juice when available. I never eat those terrible powdered eggs or the greasy railroad hash. I've learned how to trade with the other inmates so I am able to stockpile a bit of fruit in my cell. Because I have a job I am entitled to a brown-bag lunch, which usually consists of a sandwich and a piece of fruit and, on occasion something sweet. I will eat the lunch if I am able to trade for a peanut butter sandwich on wheat bread. If not, I will give my sandwich away to some poor unfortunate who still hasn't been assigned a job and receives no lunch. I then just eat the fruit. The sweet is easy to trade for something more nutritious. For dinner I usually eat vegetables, rice, and bread, except when they serve Mexican food. Then I eat my fill of tortillas, rice and beans. Once a week my cellmate makes beans, and we buy the bread that we keep in our cell with packages of cigarettes, the medium of exchange in these places. I'm losing some weight but that will level off.

I try and keep in mind that there are people on this planet who have much less to eat than I, but that thought always reminds me of when I was a kid and my mother used to encourage me to eat something I disliked because there were little children in other countries who had nothing. I could understand the message she was trying to impart, and I honestly felt sorry for those other children, but it didn't make the food taste any better.

A wonderful thing happened to me last week. My grandmother, who is bright and lively, and still lives in Colorado, has begun to carry on correspondence with me each week. Although she is in her eighties, she writes of the happiness and love in her life, and the whole cell lights up with the zest she has for all the human race, especially our family. In one of my previous letters I added a postscript asking her please to send me some pictures. I am starting a family album, having everyone send me pictures, then spending enough time studying each individual in each photograph to learn how much I care for, and love that person. I am writing those feelings under that person's photograph so that when I look through the album each day I will be reminded of the love that exists in my life. A little corny, but love is in short supply here. I need to manufacture visual reminders.

Grandma completely confused me before I could begin. Instead of sending me photos of her, my grandfather, and the rest of my family in Colorado, she sent two pictures of me. One was taken when I was about eleven years old in my Boy Scout uniform. The other was taken when I was about fifteen years old, with a friend, holding fish that we had just caught. The guard who reviews the mail must have died laughing when he saw the picture of a Folsom inmate named Maddog in a Boy Scout uniform. I've been reflecting on the incident and have come to realize how much my Grandmother and I love each other. When I ask her for photographs, I assume she will send me pictures of her and grandpa when he was alive, because I love them. She loves me, so she interpreted my request to mean that she should send photos of the person she loves, me.

What I think I've learned is that it's impossible to communicate with another human completely, no matter how close the relationship. I must give and receive love without listening too much to what words are being said and without talking too much, in an attempt to make myself understood. Strangely, I am attaining a certain love and peace through this whole bizarre set of circumstances, even here at Folsom

After returning from work each evening I have begun a ritual of taking a nap, then closing my eyes to meditate for whatever time it takes to clear most thoughts from my mind. My cellmate usually is watching television with his earphones on, so the tomb I dwell in is very quiet, almost a screaming stillness. I sit in the corner of my bunk overlooking the cell, feeling incubated in a large granite egg, with the album on my lap, pen in hand, waiting for an inspiration.

My first photograph in the album was of Ginger; glued all by itself in the middle of the front page. My hope was to write underneath the picture some new revelation as to my love for this lovely lady who I have chosen to share my life. A few days ago, while in this euphoric state, I drew a small, simple heart under the picture. I watched with fascination as my hand moved without any thought or guidance. I wrote within the body of the heart: Chick Loves Ginger.

I was startled out of my meditation. My first reaction was to laugh. No one calls me Chick anymore except my grandmother and a few aunts. I haven't used that nickname since I was in high school. What a silly thing to write. As I reflected on the incident over the next few days, I began to realize how meaningful that heart I had drawn really is. It made me become completely aware that Chick has always loved Ginger since we first met as teenagers; a simple fact that has become the foundation of my whole physical life. She has been my lover, mother of my children, companion, but most of all-she has been my best friend since I have been fourteen years old. After all these years I have tried to keep my love unconditional, striving to let it exist without expectations. Chick loves Ginger no matter what the circumstances. Ginger no longer needs to love Chick, although I know she does and always will. She can be mad or loving, times may be good or bad, it doesn't matter. Chick will always know he loves Ginger-and from that starting point I will always find a way to find peace.

I found an unused file folder and cut out a heart. After writing on it that Chick loves Ginger, I taped it above my pillow. I have made a commitment to myself that for the rest of my life, wherever I may live, I will always make these hearts and put them around the house to remind me to always keep my love simple and unconditional.

These thoughts about communicating and expressing love, got me to rethink the true meaning of Ginger and my jailhouse letters. After I was convicted and was waiting to be sentenced, we had many discussions about how we would handle living apart under these circumstances. We agreed that there would be many times during my incarceration that each of us would feel pain and blame it on the other, even though the pain would be nothing more than the problems arising out of living separately. We felt that when those times arose, we should not suppress the feelings, even though they may be false and could possibly hurt the other person, but we should write them down, put the letter in an envelope, and send it off. We agreed never to apologize to each other about what was said in those letters. The only condition we would impose was that we would write on the outside of the envelope the words "Jailhouse

Letter." Upon seeing the warning on the envelope, the other person would have the option to read it or throw it away.

Since being down (that's prison slang for being incarcerated) I have sent one jailhouse letter to Ginger and have received two. I know intellectually and in my heart that when I receive a jailhouse letter, it is the highest quality of love letter a person can receive. When things are going wrong it is usually the person you love to whom you vent your anger, not the outside world. I feel more safety in telling Ginger how much I detest the violence I see everyday than I do in discussing it with anyone living at this place. My one jailhouse letter was written after a particularly bad day, not only of violence, but of the total disregard, or what seemed to be disregard, by the guards of the suffering happening around them. The brutality that day, on both sides, broke even the most menial rules of human decency. I was upset and mad, so I vented my anger at Ginger for some piddling little thing she had forgotten to take care of for me. I was sorry I wrote it, but thankful I had written "Jailhouse Letter" on the envelope. I threw the first jailhouse letter I received in the trash, but could not resist opening the second and reading it. I sure wish I hadn't. I was so certain that I had reached a lofty place in my life where I could accept letters that come in the form of hurtful nonsense, that seems to find their way through your whole body all the way down to your entrails, as true love letters. I was wrong.

I need to keep a more watchful eye on my daily thinking and be more aware of the madness that is taking place around me. It is so easy to fall into a prison attitude, where you begin to accept values, not because they are what you believe, but because they are an acceptable part of the daily routine. The other day someone tried to smuggle dope through the visiting room and was caught. When questioned-I can only assume under duress-he confessed that it was his wife who was responsible for bringing it in, and she was promptly arrested. Even a greenhorn like me knows that if you are questioned by the coppas (I just love that term) you are supposed to "hold your mud." You are expected to keep your mouth shut and "ride the beef" yourself. The news that this man "gave her up" spread like wildfire, and it became common knowledge that if anyone could get to him he would be "hit." I weighed the punishment in my mind for a few moments, then became horrified that I would even take time to determine whether the man was right or wrong, much less whether someone had the right to stab him.

Without question, the most obnoxious brutality that exists in an institution like Folsom is rape. As on the outside, it normally occurs to someone who shows fear, or is physically weaker than their assailant. From what I have observed it normally takes two different forms. It will happen to the person whose cellmate is physically stronger and has more prison savvy. They simply take the victim as their own. I have heard this situation referred to as "the punk in the bunk." The victim is locked in with their torturer and is unable to protect himself; yet too frightened to complain to the authorities. They become a prisoner of a prisoner. I'm really not too sure how prevalent this situation is, but I do know it exists. The other is the gang-bang rape. That occurs when a group corners the victim in one of the few unguarded places in the prison, such as a cell. Not only do they all rape him, but they beat him unmercifully for no apparent reason. I was having a tooth extracted and there was a young black boy in the chair next to me. I looked over and observed the bandages and swelling on his face, but I didn't pay much attention. That's a fairly common sight here. When the boy left, his dentist related to the one working on me how the boy was gang-banged and there was hardly a tooth left in his mouth from the beating. They both laughed and began telling nasty jokes about that kid's plight. Their total lack of compassion, and the lucid details related by the dentist from the boys file, almost made me vomit. While sitting there I recalled the feeling I had when I was a young boy seeing for the first time, in Life Magazine, pictures of the Nazi concentration camps. I was about ten or eleven years old, and was horrified. I remembered thinking, "How could any human being inflict such shocking misery on another? Where could

they have found guards to perform such ugly acts without compassion?"
Listening to the dentists' conversation I realized how easy it must have
been to train those people for their gruesome work. Here I was, I
thought, listening to two educated men, placed in a violent atmosphere.
Slowly, probably without being aware of what was taking place, learning not only to condone what had happened to that boy, but believing
it was funny. My blood ran cold.

I have always felt that causing physical harm to another human being
is wrong, even though I was taught as a boy that fighting was macho. I
had my share of fights, and because I have an aggressive nature and little
fear of personal harm, I usually fought well. Even so, I cannot remember receiving any personal satisfaction in those triumphs. What anyone
here, guard or inmate, receives from all this senseless brutality is beyond
my comprehension. Nevertheless, I try to accept it all without becoming
involved. Easier said than done in a place like this. It is probably the only
situation I see here that will put me into a bad mood for any length of
time. I am working hard to detach.

Speaking of violence, there was a bizarre killing here the other day in
one of the other cellblocks. I saw the weapon when it was brought into
the captain's office where I work: a homemade spear, a really nasty looking thing. It was a shank attached to a long pole. As the victim walked
down the walkway on the third tier, he was stuck with the spear in the
throat from inside a locked cell through the bars, then was pushed by
his assailant, spear and all, over the railing. He was killed either by the
spear or by landing on the concrete three stories down; I'm not sure. It
was done so quickly that the guard walking along the catwalk a few feet
away was unable to react, or see who did it.

How senseless it all seems. Last year at Folsom there were from 350
to 400 stabbings and killings. That's over 15 percent of the total prison
population. That does not include fights, gang-bangs, rapes, and
assorted miscellany. I never cease to wonder. How did this affluent,
supposedly Christian society create all of this? I have the distinct feeling

that one of the reasons is that this very same affluent, Christian society takes little or no responsibility for creating any of this. The one thing that strikes me while meeting the inmates housed here is how few truly educated and wealthy persons reside here. I wonder where those people go when they commit a crime? Maybe they just never commit crimes? Naw! I've met too many of them to believe that.

Writing a book in this cell is really a gas. It's so quiet; the only disturbance is either the sound of the rain falling on the roof or the flicker of the images in the mirror from my cellmate's television below. I smuggled in my picture window a few days ago and it's just like being at home. The picture is of a green field with trees in the background. It hangs at the end of my bed. The arts and crafts people even painted two small children standing waist-high in the tall grass, looking at the trees, holding hands. It's like having grandchildren standing in a field just outside the door. I think my cellmate is even impressed, but change comes hard in a joint like this. I tried negotiating for the potbellied stove with arts and crafts but came up empty. It is tough to get anything accomplished if the project might not be labeled "cool". Reputations are always on the line. I have to dismantle the window scene each morning before leaving for work, and hide it or it will probably be confiscated. It's worth the effort, such small pleasures are hard to come by.

Now that I'm getting comfortable here, the authorities are discussing transferring me south to Chino State Prison, in the Los Angeles area. It is a minimum security facility and, I would imagine, much safer for someone like me-but I have the feeling I will miss Folsom. It sort of grows on you. (I know, I know, so does fungus.)

I have yet to explain why I was sent to Folsom, a maximum security prison, when the crime I was convicted of was a minimum security, white-collar crime. Well, to tell you the truth, I didn't mention it because I haven't the slightest notion why. I'm certain it had nothing to do with the fact that I made the justice system take me through a long, drawn-out trial rather than plead guilty. These nice people wouldn't possibly regard my stay here as a penalty for demanding my constitutional right to defend myself, would they? There certainly were a lot of people who were irritated.

The California Department of Corrections classifies an inmate by a complicated formula, assigning points to the individual for the severity of his crime, how many terms he has served in the past, the violence associated with the crime, length of the term to be served, and so on. The minimum number of points required for the Department to classify a person to Folsom Prison is sixty. Most inmates far exceed that amount. For instance, one of the people I work with, a nice enough guy, told me he has 302 points. I have 12. When I mentioned this fact to someone when I first arrived, he looked at me in amazement and said, "What did you do, rob a candy store?" I decided to keep the number of my points a secret from that moment on. Especially since I now have the handle of Maddog. When the classification board brought me into their meeting and told me they had assigned me to the Folsom mainline, they waited for a few moments to let me absorb the impact of their decision. I had the feeling they expected me to roll on the floor, begging for mercy, pleading with them to have the compassion not to send me to that terrible place where grown men are raped and pillaged, stabbed and strangled. They were as melodramatic as the Kid. Ginger visits me each week now, and her visit has become my weekly highlight. We are now able to be with each other in the visiting room and actually touch, rather than look at each other through the glass and converse only on the telephone. The visiting room is small. Everyone sits on folding chairs, auditorium style, while the guards sit in the front to have a clear view. Ginger and I hug and kiss. I think I rankle some of these crusty old guards with my behavior. After all, that type of conduct should be beneath the dignity of hardened criminals. The sad part is they really believe that nonsense. They might possibly take away my handle of Maddog if I continue. Nevertheless, we hug and kiss. Then she buys me a sandwich and a Coke from the machine. We talk a little. We hug and kiss some more, then she buys me some candy and another Coke, and we talk again. Then we hug and kiss again, eat and drink again, until visiting time is over, and they come and pry us apart. Then we hug and kiss goodbye. Did I mention how much I love Ginger? If I have, forgive me; I just love repeating it. This whole thing has been such a strain for her, even more than it has for me; yet each time she visits she walks through the door beaming, creating the illusion that she has wallpapered the stark granite walls with bright-colored, flowery murals. She clearly shows the strain she is under, though. At first, it surprised me because I wondered why would she be under a strain? I'm the one in prison. She no longer lives in the house and has moved in with my oldest daughter in the Bay Area; trying her hand at going to work, selling carpet commercially. I think she is doing fairly well considering this is her first real job on her own since we were married. So what can the problem be?

I have given it a great deal of thought because it simply made no sense. It occurred to me that it was necessary to show more compassion for what is happening in her life. I'm realizing that I dwell on my own situation without much consideration for her feelings. When I think about the truth of our life, being here is unique for me, to say the least, but all my life I have had to cope with tough problems in one form or another in the nasty world of commerce, while she has been home caring for me-actually putting up with me-and providing a loving home for the family. Most of her life experiences didn't equip her to face what is happening now or what occurred over the last couple of years in court. This has turned her whole world upside-down, and I am slowly understanding that the one who has taken the worst beating in this whole affair is she. I am trying to do what I can. It's too easy to sit on my duff and tell myself that since I'm locked up, I am unable to do anything to help her situation. Once I laid aside my own little daily problems, I found there were several things I could do. First, it is

within my ability, and therefore my responsibility, to provide her with
emotional support. Not only by telling her how much I love her in my
letters and our visits, but through lending encouragement and support for her new and, I'm sure, very scary employment position.
Next, I can relieve some of her anxiety for my situation by staying
positive. Finally, each morning after my daily meditation I ask my
personal God to watch over her. It doesn't sound like much, I guess,
but it's a start. Hopefully, during this seeming winter of our lives, I
can become more and more aware of her problems, especially once
I become settled. In all honesty, it is difficult to focus on any other
problems but my own. Admitting that makes me very ashamed of
myself. I am aware that at times I find that the elimination of the
feelings of loneliness becomes a full time job. How foolish that is,
though, because my loneliness only subsides when my heart reaches
out with compassion for someone else. I hold no illusions, creating
a stable life in here is difficult, but far from impossible. I have
absolutely no intention to give up and let my keepers put my mind
in the same prison they have locked my body.

Winter is ending and it will soon be Easter. I remember the Easter
party at my home two years ago, following our arrests. That was
when I began to realize that I was becoming obsessed with the game
of Cops and Robbers. I guess I should have pled guilty then. No, now
I'm lying to myself. I don't think I ever believed that was the thing to
do, even when the obsession started to lift. For a short time guilt or
innocence ceased to be a factor for either side; all that seemed to matter was winning. No one cared who was wounded in the battle as long
as our false pride and egos were satisfied. On Easter morning I heard
the rustling of the leaves, just as Skeeter foresaw, yet I chose to ignore
the warning signs I knew so well I knew better than to let myself
become involved in such a crazy game. There was very little I could
do to change the course of events. Oh well, had I pled guilty I would
have missed Folsom, and that would have been a shame. Just think,

for the rest of my life I will be able to walk around with the name Maddog Costanzo. If I fudge somewhat, I will be able to say that I legitimately earned the name at Folsom Prison. Cagney or Bogart have nothing on me. I think I'll start calling the guards coppa.

# CHAPTER 10

# The Truth

Enough of granite walls, back to the obsession.

After the incident in the judge's chambers, Ginger, Julie, and I stopped for dinner at a nice restaurant on the way home. I was wretched company. I thought the food and service were terrible. Ginger and Julie seemed to enjoy their food and chatted about art, as usual. I didn't want to hear or participate in the conversation. All I wanted to do was feel miserable, and I was doing an excellent job of that. I had the impression that both women knew my condition and were avoiding any mention of the afternoon's events, hoping I would not start a long dissertation about what a loser I was and how my lucky star had burned somewhere in the atmosphere, how I had spent a week fighting and struggling only to be thrashed, whipped, and beaten by an inferior foe. Oh! Had they only listened, they would have heard self-pity performed by a master.

Probably somewhere in their lives they had already experienced my high drama and decided to forgo that evening's performance. I was left to sulk by myself. As we proceeded home, Ginger mildly suggested that I attend a meeting of the twelve step program I belonged to since giving up alcohol. Perhaps sitting around talking to people might put me in a better mood. She prefaced her suggestion by remarking that I looked somewhat tired, never leaving an opening for me to launch into my prepared tirade. We had moved to this area only a few weeks before and these people were relatively unknown to me, so my enthusiasm for

Ginger's suggestion was exceeded only by my own self-pity. I moaned and groaned, but in the end decided to go.

I listened to the group discuss how much better it is to feel good than to feel lousy, and I certainly had to agree. Others discussed the rewards of helping other people with their problems rather than sulking about your own. All the while I felt that someone must know what is going on in my life and is directing this discussion to me. As they spoke I remembered that wonderful time over the first few years after quitting drinking when I spent hundreds of hours, actually most of my waking day, working with other recovering alcoholics and drug addicts, trying to help them rid themselves of those terminal addictions so they could gather the remnants of their lives back together. That was probably the happiest time of my life. I returned home with a better attitude and apologized to Ginger and Julie for my terrible behavior at dinner. I got a couple of hugs in return and my disposition turned around completely. Twelve step meetings usually have a way of helping me become quiet, listening to more positive viewpoints, and putting my life into prospective. That evening I finally began to come to grips with the obsession, and had a desire to deal with it.

My first thought on awakening had nothing to do with Cops and Robbers, either. I knew precisely what I needed to do even before having coffee. I rolled out of bed, went over to the bookcases, and pulled out a spiritual book that I had read each day for many years until I became busy dealing with the "realities" of my life. I brought it back to my bed. I wanted to begin this day with the passage I had started so many happy days with in the past. The book opened automatically to the page containing the passage verifying the fact of the numerous times it had been opened at this place. Before beginning reading I closed my eyes and tried to meditate for five minutes to put me in a receptive mood. Although I was out of practice and my thoughts would drift off, when I finally opened my eyes I felt a reasonable sense of peace. The part I wanted to read in the book was highlighted in yellow:

"In thinking about our day we may face indecision. We may not be able to determine which course to take. Here we ask God for inspiration, an intuitive thought or decision. We relax and take it easy. We don't struggle. We are often surprised how the right answers come after we have tried this for a while."

I said a short prayer for help to make me begin living my life on that basis. I picked up a pencil and a piece of paper by the side of my bed and wrote the first thing that came to my mind: stop fighting. I tried not to analyze the meaning. I jumped out of bed, put on my running shorts, did some stretching exercises, then went outside and ran an eight-mile course through the Sierra Nevada foothills around my house. It was still early so there was a cool breeze blowing, and since I hadn't worn a tee shirt, the wind felt chilly against the sweat that formed quickly on my chest and back, stimulating me to run at a fast pace. The dew was still on the grass, and the trees reflected greens and blues off the rising sun where they hung over the pathway as I ran. My breathing was easy and the glorious feeling put me into a state of ecstasy. I sprinted the last couple hundred yards, and when I ran the last few feet I threw my hands in the air, Rocky style! I was laughing out loud. I remember wishing I could find a way to explain a totally natural high, maybe even bottle it, but I knew it must be experienced. I also knew what to do to experience a natural high on a consistent basis, as I had done in the past; I needed to revive my mental, physical, and spiritual disciplines, which I had all but ignored for the last two or three years. During those years I lost sight of the fact that when I had maintained these disciplines, feeling great was a daily event. I couldn't explain why I had stopped.

I walked for another half-mile to cool off and sat on a huge rock overlooking the little valley where I lived. Beautiful homes sat on five and ten acres, containing big oak trees, horses, pools; "The American dream," I thought. "So far from the Mission District in San Francisco. So how have I become so undisciplined not to appreciate the gifts I have received in life?" My mind began to reflect on the disciplines so long neglected. I have always found mental discipline to be easy, using my good work ethic and a love for reading. I know I'm an excellent listener, too. But, like the police officer in Monterey, some people with little to say still enjoy talking. I know I'm much the same. I always run into trouble by becoming bored and then abrupt. I can remember attending all those different seminars on accounting, real estate, and a myriad of other subjects over the years, sitting there listening to a speaker say the same thing he had said an hour before. I usually left most of them out of sheer boredom halfway through. I recalled someone saying that seminars are staged to provide people who liked to talk but not work with people who like to listen but not work. Cops and Robbers had been an all consuming game that cut heavily into my mental discipline.

I glanced down at my strong legs and thin but muscular body. The benefits I had received from the physical fitness program, started so late in life, were a constant wonderment to me. As a young person I was a much better-than-average athlete; but between the ages of twenty-five to thirty-five, my major exercise was bending my elbow with a glass in my hand, or shaking liar's dice in a screaming bar while smoking pack after pack of cigarettes, so my body quickly deteriorated . After giving up alcohol I began to overeat and I got fat. When I turned forty, I decided to become an athlete again. The road back was long, hard, cruel, and wonderfully exciting. I was forced to lose eighty pounds, completely change my eating habits, give up cigarettes, and learn to run. Losing the weight and changing eating habits was difficult. Stopping smoking was easy, since I used the same principles I had used to quit drinking. Beginning to exercise took a little time. I read every book or magazine I could lay my hands on, trying to find a softer way to help a middle-aged person with disabilities to exercise his body. I did have legitimate disabilities other than the grand mal seizures. Over the years the vertebrae had begun to fuse in my lower and upper back, and at times the pain was awful. Losing the weight helped, but the pain persisted. Pain pills were out of the question because I was more afraid of becoming hooked on prescription drugs than I was of the pain. I finally stopped the self-deception, realizing that I would never get much exercise by reading books, put on a pair of running shoes and ran to the end of the block and back. I almost collapsed from exhaustion. But once I had begun the running program I refused to be deterred. Trying to adjust my speed to coincide with the proper heartbeat was almost impossible because I was so out of shape that just rising from a chair would send my heart beating into a frenzy. Over months, then years, I continued to run almost every day.

Sitting on that rock, breathing easy, I found a great deal of satisfaction in being able to say to myself that I have become an athlete again. The pain persisted, but I didn't feel it very much, certainly not the way I had in the past. I knew that when I became lazy and stopped working out I was much more aware of the pain. I had always declined to draw conclusions from that phenomenon; instead I tried to continue to work out on a continual basis. That only seemed practical since the pain would usually bother me more than the exercise. The game of Cops and Robbers was beginning to rob me of my desire to run on a consistent basis, and I knew it was only a matter of time that this obsession would completely eliminate my physical program altogether, too.

I smiled at all the mind manipulation I was handing out to myself. Focusing on the mental and physical discipline in my life was necessary, of course, but I knew without question that spiritual discipline was the mortar that held all three disciplines together, molding them to create one force. It was the most precious and also the most fragile of the three. A gift that, although received so easily, produced such dramatic changes in my life. I was beginning to become honest enough with myself to realize that for a very long time my spiritual discipline had been nil.

I stood on the pathway before I went into the house thinking how, after becoming sober, I began to acquire a special ability to remain happy each day, no matter what problems I faced, through the process of the Twelve Steps. After a few years I began to think that the happiness was a right rather than a grant; a gift bestowed on me conditionally requiring daily nurturing. Inevitably, while experiencing a more peaceful existence then I had ever known, I decided that my life had improved sufficiently so that I could strike out on my own, deleting my daily spiritual nurturing routine. Soon after, I lost that special grant-well, maybe I didn't lose it, but I sure misplaced it-and I realized that I was returning to that frightened and sick person I had been before I gave up alcohol. I was no longer drinking, but I was feeling the same excruciating emotional pain. Because of my self-will, at times my great big house with its swimming pool would become that little ugly rented room back in Mill Valley. I had forgotten the important lessons of love, compassion, and giving that I had learned in those simple Twelve Steps for living.

I remembered the joys and benefits I had received in previous years from the hours I had spent working with others, receiving in return a sense of fulfillment and serenity. I once had the honesty to realize that no matter what disaster happened to be taking place in my life, it was always caused by my own actions, not by others'. I had lost that honesty somewhere, even before the game of Cops and Robbers began. I said a prayer to just try and live life, even if not always successfully, with the thought of loving other human beings, expecting nothing in return. I was sure that was the life I wanted to live again and was fully aware that getting there would not come easy. It would require my working the Twelve Steps again from the beginning. Upon returning to the house I showered, dressed, and ate breakfast. I had made the decision to begin working with the cloak of my twelve step program around me again. Just making that decision was all I needed to do for the time being. Rather than try to figure out what to do, I decided to wait for an inspiration or intuitive thought that would direct me as to the best course to take over the next few days. I went into my library to spend the day cleaning up the mounds of unattended work I had been ignoring while living in the obsession. The desk was piled high with bills that needed to be paid, unanswered correspondence, and assorted junk that had accumulated because I had not given time to taking care of the mundane daily chores of living. Dorothy poked her head in the door and told me there was a telephone call on line two from someone by the name of Larry. The only Larry that came to mind was my son-in-law and I was pretty sure, after the events of last week, it wasn't him. I picked up the phone and said hello.

*A mild voice on the other end of the line replied,* "Hi, Frank. My name's Larry. I met you last night at the meeting. I was that little guy dressed in jeans and the pink cowboy shirt. With the white beard."

Wow! What a break!" I thought, "Here I am, trying to reestablish a new program of working with others, and right out of the blue someone calls needing some help." I was positive that helping others would help me too. I remembered him. Who the hell could forget that pink shirt? I said to my unexpected caller, "Yeah, Larry, I remember. What can I do for you? Can I help you with anything?"

"Actually, Frank, thanks a lot for the offer, but that isn't exactly the reason I called." He sounded somewhat condescending so I had trouble understanding the motive for the call. "You see, Frank, I saw you last night at the meeting, and you looked as though you could use a friend. Your face was drawn and, quite frankly, you looked as though someone had just put you through a meat grinder. I thought I'd give you a call to make sure you were okay."

All at once the tears came to my eyes. He had completely blind sided me. Over the years I had gotten into the habit of trying to help other people, but I never expected someone to call me offering assistance. I realized in an instant that it was I who needed help, just as I did in that little room in Mill Valley. I had become helpless in a raging storm of obsession. All the emotion I had been feeling for so long seemed to come flooding out. The tears were rolling down my cheeks. I almost dropped the phone, I was completely overcome, and I realized the meaning of what I had written that morning: stop fighting. I had to stop trying to control all the events in my life. If I did, whatever problems I did have would clear up naturally. I struggled to regain my composure, although I have no idea why. That little man with the white beard was patiently waiting, and I never questioned the fact that he was completely aware of what was taking place on my side of the phone. He had probably been in the same place at sometime in his life when his own little man with a white beard had phoned him, unannounced. I mumbled something to the effect that I would love to talk but could he give me his number and I would call right back as soon as I finished some important "stuff" that I was doing right then

After hanging up the phone, now crying unashamed, I went over to the couch, sat down, and sobbed for the next half an hour, feeling completely drained of all my pent-up emotion. I walked to the desk, put my head in my hands and tried to meditate, inviting God into my life, and began to experience a profound spiritual mood more acute than I could recall since the day I decided to ask for help in that dinghy little room so many years before. I picked up a pencil to write the first thoughts that came to me, hoping that my God would help me put on paper the real truth of the madness that followed my decision to fight after hearing that Ginger had been arrested. I was searching only for the truth, not what I personally perceived it to be. The truth that only comes from the Spiritual Power in my life. I wasn't sure of much, but I was absolutely positive that anything that I had told myself while involved in the game of Cops and Robbers was distorted with my own emotion and perception of right and wrong. I had to have spiritual help to find what had really taken place, and I knew that would come only when I discarded right or wrong and good or bad; when I achieved the ability to let my God speak through me on the paper without emotion. The truth is simply the truth. It is what happened, without judgment of the colored version that my mind wants to hear. I wanted to admit, as the First Step suggests, that I was powerless over this obsession for the game of Cops and Robbers; but that admission would come only when I was able to let God put in front of me, on that paper, the truth of my own actions.

Events of the past few months materialized on the paper, ones that I was aware, but I was suddenly seeing differently as I wrote:

On Easter I was given the intuitiveness to see that I was lying to Ginger. My life was truly full of good things. Still I chose to ignore that inspiration, even after witnessing at the party that day the wonders I've been blessed with, and I continued playing the game.

In Colorado I professed to tell Ginger that I intended to see how things developed, and if they became bad I would plead guilty, when all the while I intended to fight.

Last week I intuitively knew, out in the hall, that I should leave things alone and let Fred handle it all. Yet on Thursday I blew up in the court-room. That episode in the judge's chambers was simply abominable, and I'll probably end up in jail because of it.

I was shocked at how thoroughly the game had taken over my life! I said to myself, "I am truly powerless over this game of Cops and Robbers."

After saying that I became pensive, convinced that I had been living my life completely on self-will. I knew by admitting I was powerless over this crazy game of Cops and Robbers that sooner or later the obsession would be lifted. I would continue going to court, but I would try to accept what was happening around me rather than attempt to control the course of events. I wanted to trust my God. I realized once again that there are only two things I truly know about God: there is One, and I'm not Him. I picked up the phone, called Larry, and asked if we could meet. He wasn't in the least surprised to hear me reaching out for his help and, after giving directions, said to come over to his house right away. I did and we talked all afternoon and into the evening. His friend-ship, compassion, and advice were comforting; the kind of comfort that I sometimes felt as a child entering a church with a troubled mind.

That evening, after returning home, I went to my library. After meditating for five minutes once again, I began to write, hopefully with the guidance of my Higher Power, how I had been treating everyone around me: Ginger, my children, Fred and even my son-in-law. The Golden Rule had ceased to exist for me in the depths of my obsession. Throughout my sober life, my treatment of others had been the yardstick for a happy, manageable life, and it was obvious from what I wrote that I was treating all the human beings in my world with very little love and compassion. My conduct over the past few months had been atrocious-but it made me realize, also, that this situation had existed long before the arrests. I became painfully aware that over the years I had drifted away from the twelve step program that had brought me so much joy and I had tried to use material possessions and business as a poor substitute. Faced with the truth of what I had become, I felt very ashamed of myself, but under the circumstances as they existed, it was easy to admit, as the first step also suggests, that my life had become completely unmanageable.

# CHAPTER 11

# *Sanity...*

I was up early the morning following Larry's phone call. I read my little passage in the book, meditated for five minutes with much more clarity than the previous day, then wrote on the sheet of paper the first thing that came to my mind-one word, peace. Again, I put it aside without any worry as to its meaning. During my morning run my body was gliding; it felt as though my legs and arms were my body's only moving parts. My whole attitude toward the way I wanted to live my life had taken a 180-degree turn over the last 36 hours.

Court would resume in the morning; would I go back, forget about what had happened this weekend, and become caught up in their silly game again? Or would I have the ability to detach? I knew that today, right now, I had to begin a new program of spiritual discipline, one that would help me focus on the beauty of my life rather than that dung heap I had been rolling around in. I was convinced I was suffering from another obsession, but I thought addiction to Cops and Robbers certainly was not the same as addiction to alcohol. I began to think that taking the time to go all the way through the Twelve Steps didn't seem necessary. Admittedly, things were a bit crazy, but I was not sitting in a little rented room waiting to die. Things had changed. I had taken the First Step yesterday, admitting I was powerless over this stupid game of Cops and Robbers, I thought that should suffice.

I caught myself and recognized the foolishness of my thoughts. Friday evening I was a raving psychopath, flipping off the District Attorney in the presence of the judge. I marveled how easy it is to rationalize the gravity of what had occurred as soon as I began to feel better. I decided my best course of action was to complete the Twelve Steps as thoroughly as possible, and I began to think about the Second Step: *Came to believe that a Power greater than ourselves could restore us to sanity.* My mind wondered back through the years when I first taught how to do the Second Step. I've always seemed to know what insanity meant. Most of my adult experiences before gaining sobriety were obviously insane. I played the game of Cops and Robbers with an insane fascination. The madness I experienced in the county jail, most stories in the daily newspaper (except for the comics, of course), the miser who hoards his money or the gambler who recklessly throws it away, the smoker puffing the life from his body, self-righteous politicians with their endless compromises who ignore the poor and needy; all easily recognizable examples of insanity. But what was sanity? I didn't have an answer. I thought that maybe it had to be experienced to be recognized, and my problem was that I had never experienced it. I wondered, would I ever believe that I could be "restored to sanity," if I hadn't the foggiest idea what sanity means? How could I be restored to something I never had.

I decided to stop all that heavy pondering. It was Sunday morning, and I would finish my run, take a shower, eat breakfast, and read Prince Valiant. Larry and I met again that afternoon. On the day before, I had related what had been taking place recently in my life, so now I decided to hold nothing back and gave him a thumbnail sketch of my whole life to date. Upon hearing the details he agreed with my theory that a person would have to experience sanity to recognize it, and that my knowledge and skill in the area of sanity was very limited. Being an honest man, even if he did wear a pink cowboy shirt, and looked as though he sold used cars for a living, he confessed he was not the world's greatest authority on the meaning of sanity, either. We both decided to begin the search for sanity, trying to experience it together, through working the Twelve Steps, somewhere down the line.

I told him the story of my original experience searching for the meaning of sanity when I worked the Second Step after I had finally stopped drinking: My sponsor and I were sitting in a booth at a coffee shop one evening after attending a meeting of our twelve step program. I had already quit drinking alcohol for about three months by that time. I had completed my First Step but life still seemed to be treating me harshly, and I was sniveling: Ginger had divorced me and left with the children. Family and friends wanted nothing to do with me. I had no job, no car, no place to live, no money and I still was sick from the effects of alcohol abuse. All of this was very traumatic, but my sponsor just continued to smile as I went about describing my tale of woe.

Finally, he stopped me midway through my ramblings and began to tell me how I probably couldn't do much about my personal problems right then, so I should continue living one day at a time. He advised that I begin working on the Second Step. "Good God," I said to myself, "doesn't he realize how desperate my life is? Can't he understand how it is impossible to think about working one of the steps, especially one that talks about returning to sanity, while I'm just trying to figure out how to survive." He persisted, and since I really wanted the peace that I saw he had in his life, I bit my tongue and listened quietly.

He said, "Frank, each day during the coming week, as soon as you wake up-wherever that may be-I want you to spend 5 minutes and meditate. Try and clear your mind completely. At the end of the 5 minutes write down one "wonderment" that has occurred in your life since quitting drinking. Do that each day without rereading or changing anything. At the end of the week spend another 5 minutes meditating, and then read what you have written. You'll find that you will be reading about hope through the wonderments of sobriety. If you really have made a conscious contact with your God, you'll understand that just seeking the wonderments in your life will lead you to believe that some-day you will not only be returned to sanity, but you will find peace."

I became totally frustrated for the first time in our short relationship. I told him that he must be crazy. Then I blurted out, "It's easy for you to say. Tonight you'll go home to your wife, and I'll be scrounging around trying to find someplace to sleep, all alone at that. Tomorrow morning I'm supposed to wake up, God knows where, feeling wretched and lonely. Then hop out of bed-if I happen to locate one-with this overwhelming desire to happily meditate, so I may write about the wonderments in my life. Man, you've asked me to do a lot of crazy things, but this is the stupidest thing I've ever heard of. What kind of word is wonderment, anyway?" I was almost at a point of hysteria as he sat calmly listening to me. I finally said, "Don't you understand, even though I am beginning to believe in a God, right now I am completely alone." I burst into tears.

He sat quietly, holding my hand, until I began to calm down. Wanting nothing more than to help me find peace from the insanity of my life. In a voice that sounded almost still, giving the impression that he wasn't speaking at all, he said, "Frank, don't you see, your not alone, you have me." My near hysteria subsided, and a wave of serenity came over me. Somehow, I have no idea why, I felt that my God was speaking to me, through him.

The next morning I woke after sleeping on a cot in the back of a dingy little half-way house. (My sponsor had offered me a bed at his home, but I declined as he had already given me more than I needed) I still felt the peace that I had experienced the previous evening. I closed my eyes, and for the first time was able to meditate, completely shutting off the world. After finishing, I turned on the bed lamp, picked up the pad and pencil and wrote:

"My first wonderment of sobriety is to realize that I have a God. A Spirit that is always with me, but does not speak directly to me, but through others.

If I listen I will hear Him use people, like my sponsor, serve as His channel to bring me peace." I began to have hope. I came to believe that this new found Higher Power would restore me to sanity, even though I had no idea as to its meaning. The problems in my life still existed, but I believed in my heart that my search for an understanding of my God would eventually show me a way to begin coping with my life without alcohol, and define for me the meaning of the word sanity. After hearing the story, Larry gave me a hug and told me that he was glad that we had met and were becoming such close friends. I said, "Me, too."

That evening after dinner Ginger, Julie, and I sat out on the patio by the pool while my son and one of the grandchildren swam. The sun was setting but it was still very warm; the hills and trees took on that blue and green color I noticed the other morning while running. Even with the noise of the two boys it was very peaceful. Ginger and Julie were having a serious conversation, and Dorothy had just come over and joined in. I paid no attention. Smiling to myself, I realized how calm and peaceful I was compared to Friday; yet there was a better than even chance the judge would throw me in jail tomorrow morning on a contempt of court charge for my silly antics in his chambers. Tomorrow night I would probably be sleeping on the floor of some jail tank listening to the sounds of television and of young kids swearing, yelling, and fighting, rather than to the soothing sounds of young people enjoying themselves in a pool with three women conversing about children, art, and cooking. "Well," I thought, "if the judge does charge me he would certainly be within his rights. I acted like a jerk. No matter what I think of them or what I believe they are doing, I simply do not have the right to act so impulsively." I said a little prayer asking my God to help me control my actions in the future, not because I might be thrown in jail, but because I didn't want to feel those feelings any longer. My mind began to drift to the possibility of serving time in prison-not a county jail, but prison. It was hard to imagine what doing time would be like. How would I react? I wasn't afraid, I knew that; I couldn't even be sure whether I cared a great deal. I seemed to be at peace with the world, right then; yet, I accepted at that moment the fact that if I did not plead guilty I would eventually end up in prison. The game of Cops and Robbers would simply chew me up and swallow me; spitting me out the other end. I was done with struggling over guilt or innocence. I was willing to accept whatever happened to me in court. My options appeared clear: I either give up right then, hoping to make a deal for a few months in county jail, or continue going forward demanding my rights, knowing the eventual results. After all, the judicial system is an adversary system, and I had made a decision that weekend to stop being a potent adversary and remain as passive as someone with my personality could be. Today I had the ability to salvage a part of the business if I was sent to jail for only a few months. The key employees were still working, and I was sure they could hang on for a short time. We had only rented the house we were living in, but we had retained an option to purchase pending the outcome of the current events, so Ginger and the family would be all right. If the court battle ended, the enormous legal fees would subside. It was only logical that tomorrow I should walk into the courtroom and plead guilty. I was finally acquiring some peace, free of obsession. Maybe I was acquiring the sanity that Larry and I had discussed.

The strangest thoughts occur when I become peaceful. I began to realized, as I sat there, that by making the decision to plead guilty I was, once again, taking control of my affairs rather than leaving the solution to God. A thought flashed through my mind: if I pled guilty, it would be a lie-not just your run-of-the-mill, everyday lie, but one designed to sacrifice the truth because I was afraid. What would I ever tell my oldest grandson to do about his own problems, many of which he brings to me for advice, if I'm willing to give up all that I believed and plead guilty just to avoid inconveniences, even if those inconveniences would mean going to prison. That thought jolted me! It was vital for me that

I always be honorable with my grandson. I would rather be an honorable convict in his eyes rather than a sniveling, free coward.

I sat back in the chair and looked at the mountains, to begin once again to contemplate sanity, and I remembered my own Grandfather, a leathery, dark-skinned, strong, stocky Sicilian who landed on the docks of New Orleans at the age of fourteen, all alone and unable to speak a word of English. He migrated north, helped build the transcontinental railroad, then settled in Colorado, working for the railroad he helped build. He finally left, opened his own businesses in various locations, and retired at the age of fifty, a reasonably wealthy man. Through my young boy's eyes, my grandfather was the toughest and strongest person in the world, and when I hugged him years later, when he was ninety, my opinion hadn't changed. He stayed in excellent physical condition by fishing daily along the banks of the rugged Colorado rivers and streams. Almost all foods eaten in his home were prepared from scratch. I did exactly what he told me to do, when he told me to do it-not from fear of physical abuse (I cannot remember him ever hitting me), but out of respect for his true strength, the gentle inner strength that glowed like an aura around him when he talked, laughed, yelled or advised. Although he seldom went to church, usually only for weddings and funerals, I never questioned that the inner strength I saw was God working in his life. As a boy, I went to Mass each morning with my Grandmother, but it was only later that I came into conscious contact with how God handled things, when I had breakfast with my Grandfather. My grandparents lived in a modest but comfortable home, using the kitchen and dining room as a gathering place for the family, whose members all lived close by. After Mass and breakfast my Grandmother made bread and would always bake one or two rolls for me. I would stand with my nose against the screen on the kitchen door savoring the smell of the still-baking bread. She would remove the loaves from the oven, cut my rolls down the middle, and spread homemade butter over them. I would throw open the screen door, rush in, and gobble them down. Not only were they as good as they smelled but the extra benefit I received was to see the delight in my Grandmother's face as I ooohed and aaahed on how marvelous it all tasted. There was an aura of God around my Grandmother, too. Everyone who ever visited their house felt their simple love. When my son was small, he took a vacation to visit my grandparents. When he returned home to the twenty-two room mansion where we lived, he looked at me and became seriously thoughtful, as only a five-year-old can be. "You know, Dad?" He said. "When I grow up I'm going to have a big house like Grandpa in Colorado." I knew exactly what he meant. All my life I had tried to create that home, but all I had been able to achieve was a twenty-two room mansion that was not nearly the size of my Grandfather's modest home. Even my five-year-old son realized that.

My Grandfather gave me many words of wisdom which I have tried to use in my adult life. One day he took me fishing in a magnificent, wild valley called Gothic, where we had to leave the car and hike the last few miles over the rough terrain. As you entered the valley the cliffs rose like the spires in some great European cathedral. A small stream ran down the center of this almost wilderness valley. Aspen trees grew everywhere. It felt as though I was entering a spot on earth where no human being had ever been, and I was in awe. Grandpa went right off fishing and I was quite sure he would be so busy I would not see him for some time. When he returned, he opened his basket and showed me how many fish he had caught, and cautioned me not to be so impatient. "Let the fish swallow the bait and the hook," he said. One time Skeeter told me that, also. I guess all older men understand that simple concept. Grandma always packed large lunches of olives, homemade bread, cheese, salami, and other assorted delicacies. Fishing in a wilderness is a hungry business.

After eating our lunch in that beautiful valley he told me a story about two freight cars of grapes. There was a time, when he was younger, that his businesses had failed and everything he had worked for during his lifetime had been lost except for an old flatbed truck. Work was scarce and things were becoming desperate. He went to the train yards to see whether there was any work. As he drove past the station he discovered two freight cars loaded with grapes, just sitting there. It was obvious to him that they would rot before reaching Denver, their ultimate destination, so he walked into the station master's office and made an offer to purchase them. He informed the station master that he was temporarily out of ready cash, but he promised that if the grapes were released to him he would be able to pay in full within three days. A reluctant agreement was reached on the terms requested. Within two days the grapes were completely sold, door-to-door in the Italian community, and I can only assume wine flowed like water. The debt was paid as agreed, and my Grandfather had secured the stake that eventually led him to early retirement and the ability to out-fish his grandson. When Grandpa finished his story, he advised me never to waste time worrying about setbacks, but always to remember to stop when there's no way out of a situation, and look for the two freight cars filled with grapes. They would always emerge if I approach the situation without fear, and with confidence in my own Inner Spirit. Each of us have magic moments in out lives, but sitting there, listening to him tell me all I ever needed to know about living a happy life, concealed in a natural setting that would rival any now existing, was a magic that will remain with me for as long as I live.

I always believed the stories my grandfather told me because he was an honorable person and deserved my respect. Sitting there by the side of the pool, looking at the mountains, contemplating sanity, I was positive that if Grandpa had come to a place where he had to be less than honorable or go to prison, he would simply go to prison. I know his grandchildren meant that much to him; should my grandchildren expect anything less from their Grandfather? "No," I said to myself, "I wouldn't plead guilty." But I did promise myself to tone it down and play a passive role until it all ended. The decision made me feel peaceful. I understood then what I had written that morning: Peace. Sanity must be a synonym for peaceful. I remembered that valley in Colorado and the serenity I felt in a wilderness with the wonders of nature and the wisdom of my grandfather. I knew that one day God would grant me peace in my life. And restore me to sanity.

When I returned to the courtroom the following Monday, the judge chose to ignore my conduct and did not slap me in the pokey. I took the little gift that was offered and remained quiet for a day or so, but I had hardly let go of the game of Cops and Robbers completely. I knew I would never let go until I had made the decision to turn the whole matter over to God, as the Third Step suggests. What a joke! There I was, having trouble making a decision to keep my mouth shut for a few days so the judge wouldn't throw me in the hoosegow, yet, if I wanted to follow the Twelve Steps as they are written, I would need to make the decision not to do anything and let a Higher Spirit handle everything. When I first stopped drinking and was at the gates of death, I stopped trying to handle the events in my life and life became better than it had ever been before, almost instantly. Still, letting go after believing for so long that I was in complete control appeared to be an almost insurmountable hurdle. The hearings proceeded at a much smoother level for two reasons: Fred was now free to represent me unhindered, and I had become relatively passive. Although by Wednesday I could feel myself drifting into the old habits of trying to control everything that was happening around me in the courtroom, and I was convinced that if I didn't make an additional effort to complete the Third Step, *We made a decision to turn our will and our life over to the care of God, as we understood Him,* I would soon lose all the ground that I had gained over the past few days in my fledgling spiritual program.

I had spent those first couple of days reflecting back to those first few months of stopping drinking. I remembered that even then I was sure that I would never be able to complete Step Three the way I was told to do it. I felt I was spiritually bankrupt. Everything I had been told by my sponsor had happened exactly as he had said it would, yet when he began to discuss partnerships with a Higher Power, I was glad no one was within earshot of our conversation, because I was sure they would have locked us up in a mental ward. He advised that upon awakening I should once again meditate for five minutes, then write in my own words something like this: God, if it's Your will, please form a partnership with me, where You become the senior partner and I become the junior partner. One where You make all the decisions. One where those decisions are shown to me in whatever form You think best. Give me the strength, willingness, and ability to carry them out. Would You also please show me when the Partnership has been formed?.

He told me that the first major decision of the partnership would be to let me turn my will and my life over to His care, as it was certainly obvious that I hadn't the ability to run it. He explained that something would happen, in the form of a spiritual experience, to show me when the partnership had been formed. He quietly related that the purpose of the Third Step was to project myself into the Fourth Dimension, without space, time, or matter. He said that this dimension always exists around me but that I needed to let go of what I perceived to be reality to achieve it. I was sure that I was listening to complete nonsense, but made up my mind to do it, if only to pacify him.

While all of this was happening, coping with my personal life still remained difficult. I was living in an old friend's house for a couple of weeks while he was on vacation, and I had the use of his car. So my basic living conditions had improved, but Ginger who had divorced me because of my alcohol problem, was getting on with her own life, working to support herself, and even dating other men. The jealousy I felt seemed to be all consuming. I was told this emotion was another obsession similar to my addiction to alcohol, and that each morning, after writing my Third Step prayer, I should write about my feelings of jealousy. When I tried to do as I was advised, the emotion was so strong that I could barely lift a pen. Nevertheless, I did begin to write about the relationship, honestly admitting that the problems that had occurred were my fault. A week passed. I began to feel some relief at times, but soon I would experience another overwhelming jolt of jealous rage and return to my emotional mire. One evening a tall thin man named Glenn-who had accumulated several sober years in my twelve step program, and who we shared the same sponsor-told me that obsessions of jealousy can, and will, be removed if I ask my Higher Power to do so without putting conditions on my request. As usual, I didn't believe him, but felt so heart-sick that I decided to follow his advice. Each evening I began to pray for this jealousy to be removed from my life for only one reason: that the emotion was an ugly obsession. Adding that the prayer was not meant to restore Ginger back to me. I cannot be sure how truthful that prayer was, especially when I first began saying it, but it was becoming apparent that the emotion of jealousy was unhealthy, and would always stand in the way of my progress of ever gaining lasting, positive sobriety.

# CHAPTER 12

# Minimum Security

*Chino Institute For Men, June 1986.* Most of California's arrests take place in Southern California because of it's greater population. The prisoner is then shipped to one of the many prisons in Northern California. Rarely is someone in Northern California-which has the preponderance of the state's penitentiaries and a lesser population than its southern constituency-shipped to Southern California. So here I am settled down at CIM, near Los Angeles, 500 miles south of my home, in a facility where you could count the number of inmates from the northern part of the state on one hand. I am slowly coming to the conclusion that either I have extremely bad luck when I am assigned to a facility, or several people were certainly dissatisfied with my actions in court before entering the prison system. Well, it doesn't matter a whole lot. My ability to do anything about it is zero. This joint is listed as a minimum security prison. We sleep in dormitories and have the freedom of the yard from breakfast to 9:30 at night, except for the times they count everyone to make sure the gang's all here. I use the word gang quite literally: this place is loaded with members of the Crips gang and the Bloods gang, fresh from the streets of L.A. and surrounding locales, as are all the Southern California Chicano gangs. Northern California Chicano gangs don't seem to be represented, since they are supposedly at war with Southern California Chicano gangs. I have no idea why they are at war and couldn't care less. Folsom had white Aryan gangs, but I don't know whether they are part of this hodge-podge. There are a great number of illegal Mexican kids, most of whom don't speak English, and a small Cuban colony whose members keep very much to themselves. I know a few. I like them.

I have observed that to be a good working member of a gang you have to have an attitude, or at least convince your homeboys that you have one. An attitude seems to be a commitment to what your particular homeboys believe in. I can understand that. My only problem is that when I overhear their conversations, their attitudes are childish. But, of course, that's the whole point; I try to keep reminding myself that most of them are little more than kids. Very dangerous kids, I will admit, especially while on drugs and holding a weapon, but they think that their only protection, both in a place like this and out on the streets, is their gang. It is their way to live somewhat better than the ghetto existence society hands them. When I speak with them on an individual basis they are mostly pretty normal kids, with hopes and dreams like everyone else, yet it appears that when they are together they share an attitude that they believe amounts to survival; so their personalities change. Well, I really find it difficult to criticize their conduct because without realizing it, during the few months I spent in Folsom, I developed an attitude myself.

When I first arrived at CIM, I was housed in a dormitory filled with young men of every size, shape, nationality, and color. Most of them had personal ghetto blasters playing as loud as they could play, and each tuned to a different station-hard rock, salsa, R&B, heavy metal. The noise level made the sounds of the county jail like an evening in a tea room with a string quartet playing Bach. It was not a major problem; if I felt overpowered, I would simply get up and walk out in the yard or just go to sleep.

One afternoon I had just returned from work, taken a shower, and was sitting on the edge of the bed tying my shoe. I slept on the bottom bunk. The young Chicano who slept in the bunk next to me walked in with two homeboys. One of them held a ghetto blaster turned on to full volume. They spoke loudly to make themselves heard over the sound of the music. Noise was something that I had long ago decided not to worry about, but in this instance my bunkmate's homie threw the radio on the bed. It landed under my nose. That irritated me. I yelled over the noise of the music and the loud talk to-please-turn the volume down. The kid turned around, flipped me off and said, with a care-less manner in his voice, "Fuck you, old man."

"Old man! Who does he think he's talking to?" I was off the bed, out in the corridor, yelling at this kid to stop hiding behind his homeboys in the aisle between the bunks and follow me into the day room. I was about to beat the living daylights out of him. I could see myself and hear myself, but I still couldn't believe I was doing this. What a stupid stunt. Fighting's for kids. I must be off my rocker. The three of them stayed where they were. The one with the radio said, "I don't want to fight you, old man. Oh Christ, I'm sorry, I didn't mean to say that again." But I was screaming at the top of my lungs for him to come out and fight, realizing that was the last thing I wanted him to do.

It ended as quickly as it started. A guard ran up, pulled me back to my bunk, and told the homeboys to leave and go back to their dormitory. I was sorry they left. It didn't give me time to apologize for being such a jerk. I did apologize to my bunkmate, though.

I was startled by my reaction. It brought home to me that no matter how even-tempered I might feel, I must continue taking daily inventory of myself to keep my life in perspective. Each morning I try to spend the five minutes of meditation to create a more conscious contact with God and read my little passage asking for intuitive thoughts and inspirations. My outburst definitely was not an inspirational thought. Later, I recalled, on that day I was late for work and didn't go through my morning routine. I'm slowly discovering that I have my own "gang"—a conscious contact with God-and that I will survive quite nicely as long as I remember that simple truth.

Here at CIM I now live in an old folks' home. Actually, it's a dormitory set up for people with disabilities. I qualify because of my back and my seizures. Most of the residents suffer from heart problems, liver problems, back problems, loss of limbs, and other maladies. We have a blind man and a man who is ninety-three-years-old. What dastardly crimes did they commit to be sent to prison? I've tried to imagine some judge sitting on his high bench, gavel in hand, hammering down the sentences of a blind man and a ninety-three-year-old, and taking some perverted pride in knowing he is serving the cause of justice. Each inmate has a single bed, a locker, and a writing table. Rules governing earphones for radios are strictly enforced so the noise level is tolerable. I've also finally now have a roaddog; an older Japanese man. He is quiet, intelligent, and extremely clean-all qualities important to me living in a place like this. I am acquiring a strange sense of serenity. I think I am accepting my fate in this unreal world of prisons, guards, gangs, and solitude.

# CHAPTER 13

# *The Call...*

*San Francisco, June 1985.* The luncheon crowd at the Fior D'Italia was quiet and subdued; old men, bankers, stockbrokers, lawyers, all conversing in controlled tones while putting together multimillion dollar deals. The waiters moved back and forth from table to table, unobtrusively serving the carefully prepared food without disturbing the minions at their handiwork. I sat in a booth I had occupied many times in the past, discussing business with some associate in the quiet atmosphere of my favorite San Francisco restaurant. My table overlooked the fountain in the middle of the dining room, where the water flowing into the pool created more noise than all the diners and waiters. I was lost in my thoughts when from across the room I heard a wonderful voice interrupt the silence.

"Hiya, Daddy!" She announced her entrance. She then moved forward as though she had just entered a New York disco looking for the action. She was dressed in a lavender dress flaring from her petticoat and she wore an outrageous matching lavender hat with a wide net brim shaped with one side folded up like an Aussie's. She was not only spectacular but beautiful. I came out of the booth immediately so I could greet her properly with a big hug and a kiss. This beautiful woman was, in fact, my daughter. How many of the old men would have sacrificed today's million just to be hugged and kissed by Janice? Much less have lunch with this vibrant and beautiful barrel of fun. As we settled into the booth, the restaurant returned to the business of business, and Janice started an endless flow of chatter about boyfriends, family, and the advertising business. After meeting with Fred all morning about the upcoming trial, listening to her was totally refreshing. I smiled to myself, thinking that, finally, I had been brought to the point where the game of Cops and Robbers held no interest. I was completely willing to accept whatever happened to me. I no longer had a desire to defend myself-yet I had no desire to plead guilty. It had occurred to me that in the end I would be the only one who was free. Even if they convicted me, I would simply go to prison, serve my time, and resume my life. On the other hand, my adversaries would continue the game of Cops and Robbers, living out their lives doing time on the installment basis.

Ginger had been released at the preliminary hearing just as the attorneys had predicted. Most of my accusers testified that they had no dealings whatsoever with her. Some even testified that they had no idea who she was. A tremendous burden was lifted from my shoulders when she was released because I was wrong ever to have put her at risk in the first place. She suffered greatly by being held hostage. Through all the remaining hearings as to my own fate, over the past ten months, she had not been able even to set foot in a courtroom. She would be staying with her mother for the duration of my trial to avoid any more trauma then she had already suffered. I glanced up from my musings and Janice's nonstop account of the upcoming trade show in which she planned to participate to realize that a waiter was standing over me with a phone. I thanked him, plugged it into the jack, and said "Hello."

"Frank," the voice sounded very emotional "This is Fred's secretary. Something terrible has happened and I think you should get back here right away. I can't say much more on the phone, but please, hurry."

What's going on? Is Fred all right? Put him on the phone." I felt my heart start to pound and knew that something awful had happened to my old friend. "Tell me what is going on, right now!"

"Please, Frank, come over right away. Fred will explain when you get here." "Good Heavens!" I stammered, thinking I had better stop arguing and leave. "I'll take a cab right away. I'll be there in fifteen minutes."

I gave Janice a quick explanation, left her some money for the check, and rushed out. The valet hailed a cab and I was on my way to face the next onslaught of the people's justice. During the ride through North Beach into the financial district and Fred's office, I thought how silly I was not to expect them to do something to Fred at this point. Why should they change their tactics now, only three weeks from the trial?

I was ushered quickly into Fred's private office. Fred was white as a sheet, as I had expected. He was in control but thoroughly rattled. We both caught our breaths, and he told me what had happened. "I got a call from the Superior Court judge who handled all the hearings last month. You remember, the arguments regarding the District Attorney's conduct when he tried to arrest me, and all the illegal search and seizure issues. We discussed some minor legal items and he seemed quite friendly." Fred's voice began to break. "Just as we were about to hang up he said 'By the way, the District Attorney was in my chambers this morning with a warrant for your arrest. After reading the charges I decided to sign it. Frank, I almost fell out of my chair, I was so shocked! I was having trouble holding onto the telephone. He sat there on the other end of the line for what seemed to be eternity-then he said, 'Just kidding.'"

That son of a bitch.

"Honestly, Frank, the impact was so overpowering I felt like I was about to vomit. After saying that, he simply hung up. The secretary walked in just at that time and that's when she called you. I was caught completely by surprise." After recounting the story of the phone conversation with the judge, Fred began to shake. I hurried around the desk to help him get a grip on his emotions, but it was obvious that this was the straw that broke the camel's back. The bastards knew all they had to do was break Fred and it would all be over for me.

This time I never hesitated. I told Fred to draft whatever documents were necessary for him to withdraw from the case. I think under any other circumstances he would have protested, but at that moment he was shaken, he was vulnerable. I knew I was making the right decision; he did not deserve that treatment. The time had come for me to protect him and no longer leave him to the mercy of the no-holds-barred game of Cops and Robbers as I had done in the past.

Fred honestly lived his life expecting justice to be served. He was willing to stake his career to prove it. I had learned to understand what Fred had been risking by his representation of me when, during a hearing in a previous month-presided over by the same judge who had made the threatening phone call-the judge ruled that if Fred gave any testimony regarding his understandably befuddled state during the week in which he was being threatened with arrest, the judge would report him to the State Bar Association for improper conduct. His reason being that if Fred did not have a completely clear head, yet continued in the case, he had a serious conflict of interest, and he should be subject to disciplinary action by the State Bar, with possible loss of his license. That ruling was convenient for law enforcement, since without Fred's testimony I could not prove that the Kid had violated my constitutional rights by menacing my attorney with false accusations. The burden of proof fell on me. I had to show that what happened those few days, while Fred was being harassed, caused harm to my defense. Fred was obviously the only one who could affirm that he was less than one hundred percent competent during that week while waiting to be arrested.

During that hearing I had no idea of what was taking place in the courtroom because the lawyers were all speaking in their legal language, so foreign to most laymen. They had to stop the proceedings so Fred could explain that he was once again being threatened, this time by the judge in a way somewhat more subtle than the Kid's threat of arrest. Inside the courtroom, that old familiar look of gloom came over Fred's face. When I finally caught the drift of what was happening around me,

I was not only not surprised, but I was resigned to whatever I was about to hear. I smiled at him and said, "Don't worry, we're only going through the motions anyway. How's that for a bad pun? There's always another day, don't risk it; give it up." He frowned and I could see he was appalled by the judge participating so blatantly in the game of Cops and Robbers. Seeing him appalled again was always a good sign.

I felt like Yossarian, the main character in Joseph Heller's book "Catch 22." He was caught up in a game, too. While serving in the Army Air Force, in Italy, during the Second World War, his choices were: accept the corruption around him with its surface benefits, receive a promotion and become a hero even though he detested the idea of heroes, go to prison for refusing to fly any more missions, or actually continue flying more missions than the amount required, risking almost certain death. In the end he tries to escape in a rowboat for Scandinavia.

My situation appeared to be: become part of all the corruption, insisting Fred testify anyway and let him take his chances with the State Bar, tell him not to testify and go to prison eventually, plead guilty and go to prison immediately, or like Yossarian, I could get into a rowboat and head for Scandinavia. My twelve step program was becoming strong again, and I hadn't the slightest desire to escape. Using a geographical cure to solve my problems never seemed to work for me because I always brought with me my only real problem: me. The longer I sat in Fred's office reflecting on that day in court, the more I was convinced that the decision to extricate Fred was the proper thing to do. It was Friday; I'd go home, clear my head over the weekend, and try to figure out my next move on Monday. Fred told me that I would have to prepare an affidavit explaining to the court the reasons I had decided to remove him. I smiled inwardly and told him I would. After all, I didn't care any more about their game of Cops and Robbers. I had turned the outcome of all of this over to God months ago, or so I thought, and now was the time to find out how well I had accomplished that step. Driving back home from Fred's office I thought how crazy the situation seemed. I was becoming increasingly tired as the months went by. They were wearing me down by the continual court hearings and the constant harassment of Fred. I felt a twinge of panic and began to regret impulsively releasing Fred as my attorney. I didn't have the slightest idea what to do to find a new one. Over the last few months my financial situation had become a little desperate. The business had folded for many reasons, not the least of which was my lack of attention. My daughter had left my son-in-law after learning he was the undercover informer; she moved in with us, along with the grandchildren. I was covering the monthly overhead, but what little we had left was dwindling and soon would be gone. I certainly didn't have enough money to hire a new attorney. I felt frightened and alone. "Oh well," I thought, "things always have a way of working out. This will all be over soon; I'll get back to work and these problems will disappear. I still know I did the right thing today with Fred. He's coming to the point where much more of this harassment and he'd fall apart. I think I should spend the weekend drafting the affidavit Fred needs to file with the court for him to withdraw from the case. But what should I say?"

Once again, I became caught up in the game of Cops and Robbers without even realizing it. A new idea appeared, rustling the leaves in that part of my mind that had created so much chaos over the years. Soon they would blow in every direction and leave me helpless and naked in a raging storm of revenge.

I thought, "I'll write an affidavit all right. An affidavit that will expose those so-called champions of the people and their methodical harassment of Fred. Then their ugly legal antics will be on the court record. I can't believe I haven't thought of this sooner. This could win it for me!" I was totally caught up; this new idea afforded me the possibility of really winning! All those solemn promises to myself and to God to continue the affair in a passive position disappeared and I abruptly took hold of the reins. I'd show everyone how I'd pull myself out of this deep mudhole. The legal chicanery of the Kid and his cronies had always galled me. The threats were always off the record. I was blackmailed into letting Fred become a witness for the prosecution to save him and, in turn, save myself; but the transcript of the proceedings would reveal only that my attorney had been threatened with arrest for complicity in the alleged crime. It would also show that his implication was subject to a continuing investigation. It would not show that Fred's ability to defend me had been impaired by the threat of his arrest without the risk of loss of his license to practice law. The judge in the preliminary hearing violated my constitutional right to an attorney by refusing to discuss the subject of my being my own attorney and, since there was no discussion, there was no record of his refusal. Finally, a Superior Court Judge, that very day, had threatened Fred very subtly over the telephone under the guise of a sick joke, and that phone call would never appear on the record.

If I were to be convicted, I knew that if an appeal court read the transcript as it was presently written it would not be aware of these pertinent matters. To them, Fred would appear to be some sleazy attorney representing an even sleazier client. Most of the information needed for an appeal was off the record. Until that moment I believed I could do nothing about it. But my affidavit would give a perfect excuse to let it all become a matter of record. I was sure that the opposition would file nothing to deny my claims; if they did, they would have to hang out their own dirty linen, which would only confirm my allegations. I was also pretty sure that the very fact that a judge would make a phone call to the defense attorney in a major case saying that a warrant for that attorney's arrest had been signed, even as some sort of sick joke, would be enough to declare a mistrial. That meant that even if I was convicted, I had an excellent chance to win an appeal if all the facts were on the record for the appellate court to read. I wrote the affidavit outlining all the circumstances, stating quite specifically that the judge's comments to Fred did not appear to be a joke, but a form of coercion. I was quite specific, and stated that I could never have a fair trial with my attorney or attorneys having to worry about whether they were going to be arrested. I filed the motion to dismiss Fred and proceed as my own attorney on June 26, 1985.

# CHAPTER 14

# A Spiritual Crisis

*Chino, October, 1986:* For the past week I have struggled with life after receiving the letter from my new attorney-to the point that I thought my God had abandoned me. For me, the sky was dark even though the sun shone brightly. The dormitory felt cold even though I knew it was warm, and I wanted nothing to do with my roaddog friend, who has been so close to me over the past few months. I've eaten sparsely. I tried to go to church but left halfway through the service. My only real activity, besides going to work, has been to walk around and around and around the track. God, how I hate those bastards who put me here! I know that's only self-pity brought on again because I ignored my program of spiritual discipline and the Twelve Steps before I even came here. Cops and Robbers was only the underlying symptom; I never dealt with the resentments I carried through it all and, as I sit here today, I realize it's almost like starting over.

Last week I was lying on my bed writing Ginger one of my impassioned love letters. It has become my favorite pastime-enjoying the solitude of my bunk while the madness, noise, and chaos of the dorm surround me. The young scooter bum-that's what you call a motorcycle gang member if you are his friend-who bunks across the corridor enjoys watching me write my little gems of love. He says at times I laugh to myself; there are moments when my face contorts with my tongue stuck firmly into my cheek, and there are moments when tears are in my eyes. I have no recollection of any of those expressions, but I certainly am aware of deep feelings stirred while I try to express the love I feel for Ginger, for my children, for my grandmother, and for certain dear friends.

I look forward to this solitude I experience when writing about love every day. I first discovered its soothing diversion in my cell at Folsom. It seems the exact opposite of loneliness. Closer to fantasy. While I'm involved in the writing, nothing else exists in my world. I am finding a creative side that I never thought existed, and I'm sure if I had not been confined here I'd have lived my whole life without exploring those emotions.

My concentration was broken when I heard a voice on the dorm loudspeaker ordering me to report to the main office to pick up some legal mail. Letters of that nature are not distributed at regular mail call because they require a receipt. I was irritated with having the important business of telling Ginger how much I love her disturbed to pick up another of the legal documents that flowed in on a regular basis from the new attorney, Barry Melton in San Francisco, who was handling my appeal. But I resigned myself to the minor annoyance, returned to the bunk, and dutifully opened the envelope. I glanced at Barry's cover letter and quickly realized that this was not just a copy of some legal mumbo-jumbo he was required to file with the court; it was more important. It contained the last thrust by my opponents, confirming they had won, once and for all, the game of Cops and Robbers.

Barry had enclosed a copy of a letter from the County Clerk-Recorder's office stating that they had received Barry's request for a copy of my motion to relieve Fred as my attorney, the one I filed exposing the off-the-record antics of the Kid and the judges. The letter briefly stated that they could not find a copy of the motion in the court file, only a copy of my affidavit. I could hardly believe what I was reading! The final two sentences of the Clerk-Recorder's letter put the death blow to any hope of ever using my affidavit in my appeal: "This written motion was not found in the Superior Court file. Therefore, our office must assume it is not part of the record."

I was beside myself with anger, barely able to function. Important documents in major court cases do not simply disappear. The County Clerk's office knew the motion existed because they had a copy of the affidavit, so its loss would be their responsibility. The Kid had a copy, no question about that, because he appeared at the hearing, so a simple phone call to the District Attorney's office would have rectified the County Clerk's error, if there was an error. The document simply ceased to exist; and with its disappearance, so did my chance at freedom.

I have been completely defeated. Now that I have the ability to admit that fact, I am going to ask God to help me write that searching and fearless moral inventory of myself, beginning today. I'll lose the appeal and be doomed to at least one more year here. I might as well try to serve it free of anger and resentment. If I can eliminate those two character defects, all of my days will begin to improve.

Still, I resented all those players in the Cops and Robbers game, even though I knew that my resentments always create emotional pain. I learned right in the beginning of my twelve step program that life is a series of incidents, none of which is right or wrong; they are simply the truth of what happens. If I can accept the truth of my life, live life on life's terms, I remain happy and free from emotional pain. When I corrupt the truth with anger, rage or resentment, it ceases to be the truth. It becomes my version of the truth. Then my pain becomes excruciating-both mentally and emotionally-and to recover from that suffering I began asking God to help me catalog my anger and rage, and to transfer my innermost feelings to a searching and fearless moral inventory-a thorough Fourth Step. The Fourth Step is specific:"*Made a searching and fearless inventory of ourselves.*" When I first tried to become sober I was told that I had to take an inventory, but I balked, made excuses, whined, pleaded, and almost fell on the floor frothing at the mouth, just to prove I didn't have the mental capacity to complete it. The newfound sobriety of those early days felt wonderful, and there were more benefits from rejoining the sober world than I had ever expected in my wildest dreams. Ginger had begun speaking to me again. The children hugged me-cautiously, at first-I was gaining weight, and my body was functioning physically. To my amazement, I found friends who cared for me even though I no longer had money, prestige, or a twenty-two room mansion. These friends didn't even drink.

So I reluctantly took the advice and attempted to write a personal inventory; somewhat less than fearless and more immoral than moral. Each night I tore up what I had written the previous night and started over. How could I put down on a piece of paper, an inventory explaining the antics of the drunken fool I had become? Only when I began to write every morning after the five-minute daily meditation (at which I had also balked) did it become easy, almost refreshing, to unburden myself of my guilt and resentments on a piece of paper. Conceiving of a God had been difficult while I worked on the Second and Third Steps, but the more I wrote during the weeks it took to complete the inventory, the closer my relationship with the God developed. When it was completed I realized that the world had become a different place. I felt I had become a member of the human race again. I had finally taken a giant leap toward becoming honest with myself. Certainly I was all the things that I had written-but I knew in my heart that I had a burning desire to change.

Since the initial call from Larry, I had become reunited with my God, and the Third Step experience that occurred while I was talking to those jail inmates was nothing less than a spiritual experience. So, as had happened so many years before, my life began to improve immediately. And-as I had done before-I began to kid myself that it was unnecessary to do a searching and fearless moral inventory to rid myself of the guilt and resentments I was carrying while playing Cops and Robbers. After all, hadn't I begun a program of working with others? Even though I did not formally complete Steps Four through Nine, over the loud objections of Larry, I did try to take a daily personal inventory and to seek a closer contact with God through prayer and meditation. Wasn't that enough?

Resentments have always been my downfall, so during the years after becoming sober, I've tried always to remember that I, not someone else, am responsible for all my problems. If I continue to harbor the resentments, continue to avoid responsibility for my actions, and to blame my misfortunes on others, I will inevitably become involved only in myself, and compassion for others will leave me. I knew that, yet, in the game of Cops and Robbers, I kidded myself that I could not complete a personal inventory because I was sure I couldn't be truthful about my resentments against all those people in law enforcement and the judicial system. That excuse let me continue the obsession, but in a more subtle way. By holding on to my resentments, I gave those very people a great deal of power over my life because of all my irrational emotion. I ignored that line of reasoning and kept promising myself that after the trial, win or lose, I would begin my Fourth Step (even at Folsom, later, it remained on the back burner, although I slowly came to realize that I was still being dishonest with myself. Still, with all the time available, I never seemed to get around to taking the inventory).

When the inevitable major crises arose, I simply was not prepared to deal with it.

*Chino, December, 1986:* Since I finally took Steps Four through Seven, my sense of humor has returned along with a bubbling enthusiasm that pervades my mind and body. I'm practicing the three disciplines again and feel whole. It never ceases to amaze me how good I feel when I thoroughly follow this simple program of the Twelve Steps, and how bad I can feel when I don't. Still, I continue to delude myself each time I recover from riding out a raging storm that my life will remain happy if I work them only partially, or not at all. It's been almost three years since I was arrested, Two-and-one-half years since I received the call from Larry, yet only now, in this unlikely environment, do I feel I am coming close to working the Twelve Steps totally and, in doing so, continuing to develop a more intimate conscience contact with God. Had I been working this way to overcome my self-will from the beginning, all the people I love would never have suffered the fallout from my participation in the game.

From the moment I began work on the inventory and put on paper my part in that foolish game, I felt an enormous burden lifting from my shoulders. Each morning I would wake at 4:30, spend a few minutes in meditation and prayer, asking for direction, and would write for about a half-hour or so. I wrote about my resentments and anger with the Kid, the Fox, the judges, and the witnesses. I wrote about the way I had used Fred and my family and other people I had come in contact with along the way. The more I wrote, the more it became apparent that what happened might have been avoided. I wrote especially about my relationship with my son-in-law and how, before the arrests, I could have done more to improve it. I wrote of how, before the arrest, I felt I was doing a good job running the business-but when anyone became critical of how I was handling things, I became angry and defensive rather than explain what I was trying to accomplish or listen to their suggestions. Upon rereading the soul searching document, I wasn't sure whether the disputes could have been resolved even if I had acted differently; but I was certain that if I had been more composed, things would not have come to such an emotional crisis. In the process of recording my actions, I realized that after they had arrested Ginger, my mentality was little more than that of some street gang member protecting his neighborhood or barrio. I treated the agents of law enforcement as if they were terrorists for kidnaping my wife, and they reacted on the same level, viewing me as a lawless desperado. Even after meeting Larry and understanding that I was totally out of control, I continued the battle at the expense of my family and my friend Fred rather than accept the inevitable conviction. It became clear, as I reread the pages, that I would never have had, on my own, the ability to admit to my part as I had done. I believed the writings were inspired by God and what I had written was the truth.

I arranged for a very old and dear friend to visit me over a weekend to complete a Fifth Step. The Fifth Step suggests that "*We admitted to God, to ourselves, and to another human being the exact nature of our wrongs.*" This time I was determined to follow the recommendations precisely, even though I was confined in an institution. Finding the "exact nature" was no simple matter under the best of circumstances. Trying honestly to admit to God, myself, and another human being enough truth to find the exact nature of why I was imprisoned, while sitting in a visiting yard, in a state penitentiary, appeared to be an impossible task. In the end we did not come up with any earthshaking new insights on what had occurred. We simply took the same facts that I had written in the Fourth Step and, when necessary, viewed them somewhat differently: It was I who ran the business with little or no respect for all the parties involved. After the arrests it was I who made the decision to fight a losing battle. It was I who intentionally created the circus atmosphere in the courtrooms. It was I who had insisted Fred remain as my attorney, preying on his ethical values with little regard for the consequences to him, and it certainly was I who, a few months before, in this oversized chicken coop, had whined, thinking God had abandoned me, after my stupid plans and designs didn't work out.

As we ended our conversation I could easily see that the problems I was experiencing were of my own making. I was ready to attempt the Sixth Step, asking God to make me entirely ready to have Him remove the defects of character that were the real reason for my predicament: uncontrollable rage when I did not have my own way; dishonest planning and scheming; an inordinate fear of failure that inevitably led to the destruction of most relationships with my fellow human beings; and mostly, my failure to practice the Twelve Steps completely and thoroughly over the past few years.

# CHAPTER 15

# The Tough Road to Sanity

Mental discipline returned the moment I started becoming rigorously honest with myself. With it returned the light-hearted attitude of the time I first attempted to gain sobriety by finding God. One morning during the week following my meeting with my friend, I was preparing to leave for work and was about to lock my locker but hesitated. I asked myself what is in there that is so important? By prison standards I was rich. Since I didn't smoke I had accumulated almost thirty cartons of Camel cigarettes that visitors had given me. The locker also contained food I'd bought at the canteen or on the black market; street clothes that I wore to church each Sunday; my radio; and, an enormous amount of miscellaneous junk gathered over time. Since the cigarettes were used as the medium of exchange, the cartons alone were worth cutting my throat for. But I thought that if someone stole the whole locker my life wouldn't change much. By locking it each day I'm letting my mentality slip down to a prison level. I put the lock on top of the locker and went to work leaving everything unprotected.

That evening, when I returned, my locker was locked. The guy who sleeps next to me told me I had left it unlocked that morning, but he noticed the error and sealed it himself. He admonished me for being so careless. When I announced that I had left it open on purpose and intended to continue doing so, he looked at me as though I had just lost my mind and shook his finger like a teacher warning a small child of his errant ways, saying, "Frank, you're in a prison with people who will steal anything that isn't nailed down whether they need it or not. Everyone knows what you have in that locker, and it won't last one hour without a lock."

"You're right," I replied, "But why steal when everyone knows they can come over and ask for something and I'll give it to them?" Actually, I was only putting him on. I knew it was much more fun to steal what they needed than to ask for it. That was just part of the game of hanging around prisons. I love doing something contrary to prison routine, it drives everyone crazy, especially the old cons like my bunkmate. I am well liked, but I think at times they believe I'm not playing with a full deck. I figured I would become the only inmate in the Department of Corrections with substantial assets-for the time being anyway-who didn't lock his locker. It would be worth the loss to have everyone tell me what a jerk I had been to leave it open, with me knowing that I didn't care one way or another. The next morning I threw the lock in the dumpster and, to this day, I don't believe a thing has been taken. But the real blessing is that my mental discipline has returned. I don't have to live my life at the level of prison mentality. I keep my priorities straight. As for physical discipline, I run each day and maintain a program of push-ups, sit-ups and chin-ups. Because the food here is about as good as cheap dog food, I've become almost a vegetarian. My weight has dropped to 158 pounds. The scooter bum told me that my friends are beginning to worry about the way I look-I resemble a walking skeleton-but I know I'm incredibly healthy. Physical discipline is much more essential in here than on the outside. I have continued to meditate and read my passage in the book, hoping to develop the ability to wait for inspiration during the coming day rather than to try controlling the events around me. I've continued to pray to my God to make me entirely ready to have the defects of character that we clarified through the Fifth Step removed, as the Sixth Step suggests. I have continued, in the areas where I knew I had become ready, to perform the Seventh Step by humbly asking God to remove those shortcomings. I have no doubt that He will do so. In this I have complete faith. I've been successful in all areas except dishonest planning and scheming, the scourge of my life. Through my daily actions in this place, it was obvious to me that I have also continued those old habits.

Sometimes you have to be careful about what you pray for. There are occasions when, even though your prayer achieves the result you are seeking, the way you receive it is not exactly what you had in mind. Dishonest planning and scheming continued to dog my daily activities in this awful place, so I persisted praying on a daily basis, asking my Higher Power to work with me on my Sixth Step and let me be entirely ready to accept things as they are without trying to change them for my convenience. It is very easy to believe I need to control events in here just as I always tried to do on the outside. The difference in prison is it's like watching my defect manifest itself through a microscope.

While I was working on this step, I had become involved in an incident involving two convicts in my dormitory whom I knew casually: one, a long-term convict of Italian descent in his early sixties who professes to have some ties with the mob; the other, a very tough Chicano in his early forties who has spent the better part of his life in institutions. The Italian and I came from very similar cultural backgrounds. We share boyhood stories of living in Italian neighborhoods filled with old men playing bocci ball, mothers cooking pasta and homemade bread, kids playing kick the can, in addition to all that other hanging around stories that fills the time and the need for companionship. Both the Italian and the Chicano once regarded each other as friends but a falling out had occurred and it looked as though it would become violent, only a few days before my Italian friend was to be released. The Chicano was about five-foot-ten, with a large upper body from working out with weights and long, black hair combed straight back with a part down the middle. He always wore a frown, trying to give the impression that he was more mean than he actually was. He tried to bully people and, because of his looks and demeanor, did a very good job of it. Until this incident, I had no feeling about him one way or another. Each day he would bait the purported mobster with nasty blurbs, hoping to draw him into a fight. I was pretty sure, even though he was in his sixties, the Italian would more than hold his own-but if a fight did ensue, they both would receive additional time, negating my friend's imminent release. The whole affair seemed foolish, and I began to work out a plan that I believed would resolve the matter, leaving them both a chance to save face. I felt they both regarded me with some respect, so I decided to intervene.

I had a pair of shoes that the Chicano liked. I decided to offer them to him, hoping to secure an armistice. When I saw him in the dormitory I offered the shoes in return for leaving my Italian friend alone until he was released the following day. Much to my surprise he became very angry and began to yell, for all the inmates to hear, "You're just a Goddamn Dago, too, and I don't like you either. If you want me to leave things alone, why the hell don't you go back into the television room and fight me yourself? Frankly, I think you're too chickenshit." I could feel everyone in the dormitory staring at me; the place became deathly quiet while they waited to hear what I would do. I knew I had made a disastrous mistake, but I also knew that if I didn't take up his challenge, living here would become impossible because the Chicano would own me. I mustered all my intestinal fortitude, looked him square in the eye, and said loudly so it was clear to all that I had not refused his challenge, "Okay, if that's what you want then let's go."

I turned and walked directly into the television room, murmuring under my breath that I think I finally understand what it will take for me to become entirely ready to stop planning and scheming. It looked as though I would need to have my head bashed in by this very unfriendly Chicano. Working the Twelve Steps when I was recovering from alcoholism seemed quite a bit easier than working them this time! Maybe I'm just more aware of my stupidity now. The room was completely dark except for the light coming from the images flickering on the television screen. The volume was as loud as it would go. Although I couldn't hear what the Chicano was saying, his face appeared to take on all sorts of contortions because of the light show from the TV. I was trying to say to him that this whole thing should stop right here, but suddenly his fists rose and he assumed a fighting stance. Without thinking I punched him as hard as I could. I threw my whole weight behind the blow and twisted my fist slightly on impact, as my cellmate in Folsom had taught me. I'm sure I caught him completely off guard because he had never regarded me as a serious opponent. Out in the dorm he was simply playing to the crowd and assumed I was too old and scared ever to think of accepting his challenge. I caught him right on the bridge of the nose. He dropped to the floor like a stone. He appeared to be unconscious.No one was more surprised than I! I didn't know what to do next. I certainly had no interest in hitting him again. If the truth were known, I had no interest in hitting him the first time. There was a sharp pain in my right hand and it felt as though it was broken. "My God, he has a hard head!" I thought. "It's only a matter of time before the guards show up, so I had better get out of here right now before I get busted." I turned and left the crumpled body on the floor. As I walked toward the door a blinding light flashed in my head from a punch he threw coming from behind me after he got up. He wasn't as out cold as he appeared to be. The whole right side of my skull felt as though someone had just hit it with a sledgehammer. I blacked out for a few seconds. The next thing I remember I was on my back on the floor, looking up at the raging Chicano. He had his fingers around my throat and was working as hard as he could to strangle me. If I ever needed an intuitive thought or inspiration it was now; planning and scheming wasn't quite working in my life anymore, if it ever really had. With more than a little desperation I reached up, took a great big handful of the straight black hair, and bashed his hard head against the stone wall close to our struggling bodies. My God! He had the hardest head of anyone I had ever met because he continued to strangle me. I bashed it against the wall again. This time he released his grip and rolled off of me, half conscious. Then it was my turn. I rolled over on top of him to do what damage I could, but by this time all I was interested in was putting a halt to the madness. Other inmates were pulling me off, yelling, "The Man is coming, The Man is coming." The last thing I needed was to be busted for fighting. I got up off of the still struggling body of the Chicano, who I was sure would end the evening with a very large headache, while others in the room whisked me away to the safety of the yard, out of the reach of the Man.

I walked around the track once to slow the flow of adrenalin and to put what had just taken place into proper prospective. I knew I was the real cause of the fight. I had, again, tried to plan and scheme to resolve a problem that was none of my business. I had let my ego tell me how everyone would be happy to listen and, of course, agree with my appraisal of the problem and its proper solution. When those plans and designs did not work out properly, I found myself, once again, in the middle of a raging storm. The time had come to be honest with myself and to admit that whatever problems I currently had in my life I had created through my irresponsible desire to control every event around me. I told my God that I was entirely ready to have him take that defect of character from me. I humbly asked Him to remove the shortcoming of planning and scheming.

I had been praying over the preceding few days to bring myself to a point where I was ready to do this. I never thought it would take something quite so drastic to have the prayer answered. God must have figured that my head was just as hard as the Chicano's.

# CHAPTER 16

# The Trial

*Superior Court, September 1985.* Three months after I filed the motion to dismiss him, Fred sat on the couch across the small conference room in John's office, fuming. We were both very tired. After all, it had taken the Kid almost a month and a half to put on his case against me and by this time, tempers tended to become frayed.

"Frank," He pleaded, "you can't do this to yourself. It's certain to end in a conviction. We've done great so far, but you're suggesting we throw it all away on your whim. We have an excellent defense planned, and the D.A.'s case is weak. The expert witnesses who have agreed to testify, along with the charts and graphs we have developed, showing the general direction of the business, should more than offset any gains they've made. Then we'll bring in the accountants to satisfy the jury that most of the money was spent repairing the real estate and we should be home free, putting it all behind us."

"Fred!" I countered irritably "How can you suggest that telling the truth is a whim? I'm no fool. I know what's at stake here-my freedom! I've sat for the last month and a half watching people parade on and off that stand, most of them telling their little half-truths, for whatever reason I'll never understand. Now I'm supposed to put on a defense that moves the facts around the same way, so a bunch of people can determine who tells the best half-truths? Put me on the witness stand, ask me any question you want and I'll answer it as truthfully as I can.

Then let the Kid do the same and-except for the admission I made to him in confidence when we decided to work out that deal-I'll tell him the complete truth too. Fred, the law says if they believe me even a little bit, even less than they believe the Kid, then they are obligated to let me go. Are you telling me that if I tell the complete truth to these people without any gimmicks, not one of them will even partially believe it?"

"Frank, you're impossible. You look like a crook and you act like a crook. You're loud and offensive in the courtroom. You're damned right I'm telling you they won't believe the truth from you."

I wish I could say that my motivation for limiting my defense to only my own testimony was due to my complete trust in God, and belief that most people will believe the truth when they hear it, but that would not be quite honest. The idea of defending myself with nothing more than a truthful statement to the jury sounded very noble, but my nobility was also stimulated by a total lack of money. The game of Cops and Robbers had ground me down to the position that I was completely broke. Ginger was living with her mother in Grass Valley, my daughter and the grandchildren had moved to the Bay Area, I had lost the house, and I had personally gotten down to the place where I was borrowing a few dollars from my father-in-law to keep going. The cost of expert witnesses and accountants was simply out of the question, and I'm ashamed to say I was too proud to admit my financial plight to Fred.

"I can't understand why I ever came back into this can of worms to try and defend you," Fred continued. "How can I help if you won't listen to reason and persist with this crazy thinking? You know what they say about the fool who defends himself."

"Fred," I was feeling better now, "you came back because you're a nice guy who couldn't leave a friend, I know that. But courtrooms are your life and you're a professional. Personally, from what I've seen, the whole system sucks, and I made a commitment to myself never to try and buy my freedom by joining the sleazy game they play. It's my life; you should respect my wishes even if you don't agree."

Actually, Fred had returned to the case on what appeared to me at the time to be a fluke, although as I reflect back I suspect that the court had applied some pressure when it became apparent that I was determined to proceed with the case alone. No one looked forward to a protracted trial with what they believed to be a complete maniac defending himself.

While I was acting as my own attorney, I had met with the Kid to determine whether there was any chance for a settlement. I offered him a compromise by admitting to being part of a transaction that could be construed a felony, by bending the law somewhat, but certainly not on the same level of the charges that had been filed against me. A false document was used to obtain a loan, and I was aware of what was taking place when it was happening. I told him that I would be willing to plead guilty to the new charge, of which I certainly was guilty, if the others, of which I felt I was not guilty, were dropped. After much haggling, the Kid called in his supervisor and after checking with their superiors, we agreed to the deal. I called Fred as I wanted to make sure that all the legal details were handled correctly, and he immediately drove up from San Francisco. I sat out in front of the judge's chambers while Fred, John, the Kid, and his boss informed the judge that the case had been settled and all that was needed was for me to stand in front of him, plead guilty to the new charge, then wait a few weeks until he sentenced me. The relief I felt was indescribable. I was exhausted from over a year and a half of constant mental fatigue. Going to jail would be a breeze after the constant pounding I had taken in the courtrooms. Was it all worth it? I couldn't answer that, but I certainly was happy not to have to go through a long, drawn-out trial. To paraphrase Winston Churchill, I knew it wasn't the beginning of the end, but it is, perhaps, the end of the beginning.

Fred and John walked out and said that all the details were completed; all we had to do was come back after lunch and go through the formality of pleading guilty. I could see that Fred was relieved, too. As I should have expected, when we returned after lunch, the Kid very sheepishly informed us that his superiors had changed their minds and decided to take the case to trial. Fred was appalled because it was highly irregular to back out of a deal once the judge had approved. I shrugged and walked out of the courtroom without flipping the Kid off. My obsession with playing the game of cops and robbers seemed to be diminishing.

Fred told me that he would like to defend me again, without a guaranty of payment, because he was sure they would chew me up and spit me out if I continued to proceed alone. I decided to accept his kind offer.

My will, not Fred's, prevailed, and it was decided to limit the defense to nothing more than my truthful testimony. Fred's explanation to the jury for the somewhat strange circumstances was that we believed a jury should hear the truth from me, warts and all.

The charges consisted of five counts of grand theft of the rents generated by five real estate projects. Two of the original charges against me had been dropped: the one involving the Monterey property, and one involving a property in the county. Since the judge exonerated Ginger at the preliminary hearing, no conspiracy charge remained as it takes two to conspire. In four of the five cases, a corporation that I personally controlled had purchased with a contract of sale a large, new, financially troubled condominium project from one of the accusers. A contract of sale is where the buyer enters into an agreement to purchase the property, but escrow does not close until certain conditions of each contract have been fulfilled. The terms of the contracts of sale in question also called for possession of the property to be relinquished by the owner. In all of the contracts of sale the condition of each agreement to close escrow was to sell or refinance the individual condominium units. Every project was in serious financial straights. Either the banks had begun foreclosure proceedings or were in the process of filing the necessary papers to do so. Most of the projects needed substantial work to even obtain occupancy permits. The original developer-the seller-had originally taken out a large loan to build the project, had put a handsome chunk of that loan into his or her own pocket, and were unable to sell the project's individual units. All five were former "Fat Cats" running around trying to shuffle the deck chairs on the Titanic. Their equity had long since been wiped out. These sellers were sophisticated real estate speculators; major real estate developers with a lot of problems but very few answers. Everyone was looking for the quick fix when they met me. I was amazed how panicked they had become. I guess over the years they had become so fat that when real problems developed they forgot how to think. I was certainly no saint but this cast of characters certainly had little room to point fingers. We were all a bunch of promoters making bad decisions in the worst real estate downturn since the depression:

Accuser#1—This pillar of the community had filed bankruptcy before I met him owing investors, the banks, and savings and loans over one hundred million dollars. (What was truly amazing was that the savings and loan was still loaning him money, through the bankruptcy court, to continue building. My deal with him had also been approved by that same court.) This person was a reluctant witness, but it was obvious to me that a great deal of pressure had been applied to have him participate.

Accuser#2—I was referred to this individual by the contractor who originally built the project and was still owed $200,000. The contractor wanted to see if I had a way to resolve the problem. After I had made the deal to purchase the property, I discovered the existence of a five hundred thousand dollar secret fund, known only to the savings and loan and the owner, in which he was drawing over twenty thousand dollars per month, but giving nothing to the contractor. (When I first met this Fat Cat, he was leaving with his family for a month vacation skiing in the Alps while still owing everyone several million dollars that was past due.) We soon had a loud falling out after I informed the contractor of the secret fund and the deal was canceled by mutual consent. There was very little love lost between us.

Accuser#3—This woman was renting the estate were she lived for nine thousand dollars per month at the time I first met her, while owing investors and the savings and loan several million dollars of unpaid loans. She was vacationing in India at the time the project was being built so had maintained very little supervision during the construction phase. She had not even completed the necessary work to secure occupancy permits to the project one year later when we made our deal. She had attempted to auction the units on an individual basis and had not received even one bid. After experiencing more financial problems in other areas, she was forced to leave the estate, take a job with me, and became the manager of the property in Monterey. She was the one who had refused to refund the deposits to the buyers in Monterey. She testified against me there to save herself, (or so she thought) so was a logical accuser in the new action after I was released in Monterey. I personally thought she was a very frightened person who had been sucked into the game.

Accuser#4—This person was a successful architect who had become tired of just designing projects, and decided to convince a number of friends and relatives that they would make their fortune if they invested with him in a project that he would build, not only design. Like most egotists, he abandoned what he did best and became a failure in a business he did not truly understand. There is a great difference in designing projects, as opposed to developing them, especially in a depressed market. A slick bankruptcy attorney talked him into filing bankruptcy for the sole purpose of having the court return possession of the property. When this was accomplished he promptly evicted the potential purchasers I had secured, canceled the loan commitment, and rented the units.

Accuser#5—This was a seriously financially troubled development/contracting company from who I actually purchased the units by closing escrow and received the deeds, as opposed to using a contract of sale. I was surprised when the Kid left this charge in the indictment, and had not thrown it out, as he had done with the other two. It was a real gamble on his part, because if the jury found that I had not committed the crime on one count, then I probably would have been found innocent on all counts. I could never imagine the jury coming to the conclusion that I was stealing rents from a project that I actually owned outright. (That shows how much I knew about what was taking place around me.) I think the Kid was forced to leave this charge in the indictment because it was the only project that was located in the county.

Somehow, during the trial, I had a great deal of trouble getting all worked up as to how bad these people had been cheated. Especially since the State Of California and the county were spending several million dollars more in court costs to prosecute me just to salve their hurt egos.

Anyone who has followed the real estate market over the years knows that given time, a bad market is eventually followed by a rising market. So after taking control of each property I made, what I thought to be, the logical move: I brought in construction crews to complete any needed repairs, and then I rented the units. I could not believe that all but one of the developers had not done the same. It was important to keep the project financially sound and buy time until it could be sold. I then began to work out agreements with some of the renters to buy the unit they were living in, using a co-signer to secure the loan. The case against me was circumstantial, mostly testimony and innuendoes designed to influence the jury to believe the Kid's interpretation of the documents. There was no real evidence of a crime-no smoking gun. The Kid's thrust was that even though the written documents did not contain the information necessary to prove the charges, it was important for the jury to consider the aggregate of proof offered in the case to conclude that my plan and design had never been to sell the units, but to steal the rents. Since it was I that was being prosecuted, the developers were depicted as poor, unsuspecting dupes who had been robbed of their life savings by this criminal of the eighties. I believe the Kid handled this part of the case quite well, except the very same case could have been made against each one of the developers. The Kid, or some other district attorney, could easily have made a case that each developer had taken capital and loans from their investors and the banks with the plan and design to extract funds for their own personal benefit before and during construction without ever intending to eventually sell the finished units.

On cross-examination evidence was introduced that several individual sales were being processed at the time I was arrested; in addition, many individual loans had been approved and more were being processed. A letter from a legitimate savings and loan was also introduced into evidence committing to fund me a loan that would have paid off one of the projects completely. Fred showed that each approved loan would have netted my company cash equivalent to several years rental.

The Kid hammered away that these sales and loans had never closed. He was correct, none ever did. My only response to this was to show the effort that was being made. I tried my best to explain in my testimony my business purposes without whitewash. I did what I did and felt no shame. I was quite specific that whatever transactions had taken place I had absolutely no remorse for participating in them. I was clear in my own mind that even though my treatment of human beings was less noble than it might have been, I was comfortable with my goals for the business. Fred's final question was to ask whether I had entered into any of these business dealings with the intent to steal the rents. I answered "No." I believed that answer was truthful. As I left the witness stand after five days of questioning by Fred and cross-examination by the Kid, I felt a great relief. No matter what transpired between the individual members of the jury, at least they had been told the complete truth, warts and all. Whether they believed it was up to them. I knew that whatever the outcome might be, I would never regret my decision as to how the defense was handled. But the game of Cops and Robbers was to be played once again, effectively sealing off any chance whatever of a not guilty verdict. The prosecution has a right of rebuttal after the defense rests its case, and since we had used only my own testimony as a defense, we expected the Kid to use very few rebuttal witnesses. We were right. Without any warning or notice, the final rebuttal witness he called was Fred. We were taken completely off guard. Fred made the usual objections because he was not notified, but the Kid was not to be denied. We recessed to give us time to bring John over to represent me while my attorney became a witness for the prosecution. Fred and I had a cup of coffee in the cafeteria while we waited, but there was very little to say. We had lost. It was now just a matter of time. The decision to allow Fred to exonerate himself by turning over his trust account records, thus allowing the Kid to use him as a prosecution witness, had raised its ugly head. Fred would have to make his closing arguments in my defense to the jury immediately following his appearance as a witness for the prosecution, trying to field the Kid's questions about being a possible suspect in the case. All his credibility as a legitimate attorney would be gone. I felt sorry for those people on the jury for unknowingly being subjected to such shabby tactics. We talked quietly, almost unemotionally, about the consequences, both knowing exactly what they were. Fred wasn't even appalled, just a bit heartsick. Who could blame him—The dignified gladiator being torn apart in the arena he so dearly loved? As for me, it didn't make much difference any more. I felt much too exhausted to have any real emotion. Instead of dealing with our original fear of what would happen if I defended myself, we had to deal with the Kid chewing Fred up and spitting him out as the jury looked on. I closed my eyes so as not to watch the indignity that my old friend was forced to suffer for no other reason then trying to provide an adequate defense for his client. For the first time throughout the whole ugly ordeal, I, too, was appalled. After six days of deliberation the jury returned a guilty verdict. Approximately sixty days later I was sentenced to four years in state prison. I must admit that I was curious, if not a little excited, to begin this new adventure, rubbing elbows with all the cons and cops.

# CHAPTER 17

# *Release*

*Chino, November 1987.* Should I just tell Ginger not to meet me at the gate next Saturday? What if she is waiting at the gate and they decide not to release me because more time has been added to my sentence? Worse! What if another agency is waiting at the gate to arrest me on another charge? My God, she'll be so upset. After all, there is no real reason for me to believe that they will release me even though my time is up. They've never kept their word in the past. Why should they suddenly change?

I'm becoming crazier than a bedbug, having thoughts like this at 4:30 in the morning; Of course they will release me. It's easy to become paranoid toward the end of a prison sentence. I'm sure they have completely forgotten me, yet my ego, coupled with a bit of anxiety, wants me to believe that the game of Cops and Robbers still rages in their hearts and minds. They're probably up to their ears in new games, and much too busy to worry about me. "God, help me to become very careful for the first year of freedom, because it is obvious that living in a place like this for any length of time makes a person completely lose perspective." What will it be like out there? I've changed, I can feel the difference in myself. No! There's no difference. I just need less from life. After thoroughly working the steps in here, I'm sure I will not function the same way ever again. God, what will home be like? Do they have small, intimate chapels like the one in here or are there nothing but churches?

Will I spend time in them as I do here? I doubt it; I didn't before. That's a shame; I've enjoyed attending church again. I really don't want to work for money but I'm sure I will. Yet, I just don't care about bills, taxes, or cars in the same way I did before. I would like to buy an old pickup to drive around and start to fish again.

Ginger has moved to Petaluma, California, and wants to settle there. I guess that's okay, but I wonder if there are any Chicanos. I can't remember. Notwithstanding the fight, I've enjoyed my friendships with them. They are family oriented. I hope I can continue my habit of avoiding television and continue writing letters. Writing the letters has been fun, and, if I don't write them, I'll stop receiving them. Oh, by the way, God, help me to continue writing Ginger love letters even when I'm living with her. They bring us close. I guess I'll have to go back to talking about what interests everyone out there and, frankly, most of it is boring. It's strange—I'll have to fit into their world. In here, I fit into my own private world. I've become used to solitude. What a silly thing to think about, but one of the first things I want to do is go out dancing. Just get dressed up and go to a ballroom. God, my greatest fear is that I will leave here and withdraw from the world. Help me not to turn my home into another prison. I completed the Eighth Step by making a list of all persons I had harmed in the game of Cops and Robbers and have become willing to make amends to them all. This wasn't as easy as it sounds. I realized after meditating that besides Ginger, the children, Fred, John Virga, and several other loved ones, it was necessary to include my son-in-law, the Kid, the Fox, all the judges, my accusers, innumerable guards, the Chicano, and any inmates who irritated me while I was being corrected by the Department of Corrections. Just to believe that any of these persons had harmed me made me harbor a resentment, and that is a complete lack of honesty on my part. I had to become willing to make amends to them all. It was mandatory for me to eliminate any resentments, always keeping in the forefront of my mind that I, not someone else, was personally responsible for what happened.

It was quite a colorful list of characters; probably the greatest lunatic in the game was sitting on the bunk, writing the list, and preparing to make amends. The Chicano was beside himself with anger; not only did he sustain two black eyes and a large headache from this old man with a bald head, but he lost face with his homeboys. I felt that he would not take kindly to my apologies. Instead, I knew he had a grand-child that was very dear to him so I bought a doll on the black market and had my roaddog give it to him, without mentioning it was from me. He was quite touched by the gesture, even fighting back a couple of tears. The next morning I said a prayer that he would be able to show the child the affection he so obviously felt rather than teach him how to be macho. I also apologized to some other inmates who were still living on the yard. In every case, I was greeted with good will and was surprised that, in some cases, the amend was reciprocated. The guards were a different story. Had someone observed me becoming involved with a coppa, both our lives would have been put in danger. It would be easy to construe that any conversations with the Man would be for the purpose of snitching. Since the amend might have created violence rather than the purpose intended, I decided to leave the whole matter to my Higher Power.

I know that my present living condition makes it almost impossible to make amends to the others on my list right now, so I will wait until I am released before attempting to ask my God to show me the proper amend due each person. The Ninth Step-making amends to all persons I had harmed-will probably take a few years considering the damage I caused, but I am fully prepared to follow through. It's funny, the few amends I have made so far have left me peaceful, with a longing to do more. Cleaning up the wreckage of your past can be a truly satisfying experience. The process of leaving has become much more emotional than I would have ever imagined. I was given a certificate in church, signed by the priest, thanking me for certain work I accomplished dur-ing my stay. What I did really wasn't a big deal and was blown out of proportion, but it was appreciated because there are very few volunteers in a joint. It's very difficult to explain how much that silly little piece of paper means to someone like myself, who through most of his life has been imprisoned in the bondage of self. It came as a total surprise. After walking to the alter to receive it, I was embraced by members of the congregation, even the young Mexican kids who couldn't speak English. I have already sent it to my oldest grandson with a letter explaining that no matter what happens to you, or where you might find yourself during life, there is always something you can do to improve the conditions of the people around you. I hope I never forget that. I have also been giving away all my accumulated possessions, which to the inmates around me is like distributing the Rockefeller fortune. The greatest prize, outside of the cigarettes, of course, was my radio, and I was offered a purchase price of untold wealth, by these standards. I decided to give it to a black heroin addict named George who has kept after me to let him have it for the last two months. George has been as good a friend as any addict can be whose addiction dictates that he rip off anyone, friend or foe, to feed his habit. My bunkmate was tearing his hair out as I handed the radio to George.

"Son of a bitch, Frank, don't you realize that within an hour he will have sold it for dope?" My friend didn't need the radio himself. He was only venting his frustrations for what, again, seemed to be the act of a madman.

"Yeah, I know, but I think he's pretty heavy into the dealers. The radio will buy him some time before they eventually come over and beat the shit out of him, again." I wasn't sure whether my thinking was too logical, but it seemed about as sound as any I had heard during the trial and my stay with the Department of Corrections. My little road-dog and I have agreed to say goodbye and go our separate ways. The close relationship created under these circumstances could never be re-created in the outside world. I just thank God that he came into my life and we helped each other retain our sanity. I will never forget him.

I realized while writing about George that I have written almost nothing about my observations of the use of drugs and alcohol in prison. It's an important issue since drugs and alcohol are readily available in these institutions and are used on a massive scale by both inmates and guards. Controlling their use is about as fruitless for the Man as it is for law enforcement on the outside. Deaths from cirrhosis of the liver and overdose occur on a regular basis. The sad part is that there are no rehabilitation programs whatsoever in prisons, although most inmates have a history of drugs and alcohol. They are simply released without treatment and are given very little exposure to any twelve step program, which is far and away the most effective method of recovery. So they hit the street continuing to drink and use drugs. I have been told, and I believe from what I have observed, that at least 90 percent of the prisoners released return to prison during the first year, mostly on drug and alcohol charges which precipitates violations of parole.

Addiction to drugs and alcohol is a terrible personal tragedy and I only have one sad story which, to me, tells the tale. It concerns a wounded Vietnam veteran in his thirties, well educated, but a hopeless drug addict. He sleeps across the corridor from me. Each week he begs the dealers to let him have some heroin, and he promises he will pay them the next day. They know from the beginning he will never be able to pay, but they enjoy the sport, so they front him a hit, and when he is unable to pay they beat him unmercifully, just for the fun of it. He is then sent to the hospital to recover. Almost as soon as he is released the game begins over again. I began to suspect that there was more to this threepenny opera than would meet the eye. It just seemed to me that there must be an easier way to get one hit of heroin every week or two than to have yourself severely beaten.

One evening he returned from the hospital, as usual, bandaged, with several black and blue marks, but appearing quite chipper. I suddenly flashed that his real motive for the game was not the heroin, although that was a real perk, but was the painkilling drugs he must receive in the hospital during recovery. The beatings provide him with an excuse to receive a steady supply while recuperating. I realized he wasn't hooked on illegal drugs, he was hooked on legal prescription drugs. It made me sick to think that he got hooked on those drugs while recovering from wounds received fighting a foreign war; yet our society's solution to his addiction is to put him in a prison with almost no facilities for recovery. What a sad commentary on the treatment of any human being, much less a wounded veteran. I gave him some advice on how to kick his habit and a telephone number where he could reach me on the outside if he survived.

Eliminating any addiction begins with a program of recovery, and the Twelve Steps have been shown to be the primary recovery program over the years. I have spoken with over 100 men during my stay, all of whom want desperately to be free of their habit, but it's like spitting in the wind. There are no central facilities for meeting together on a daily basis. Outsiders in twelve step recovery programs do come in to try and help, but it is only for a couple of hours, and their visit is hampered by many security regulations. The inmate is required to keep quiet and listen; there is no group participation. Reading materials on these subjects are nearly nonexistent, and prison policy forbids the formation of private groups without a prison official attending the meeting, thus eliminating any chance of anonymity and free discussion of problems.

I usually worked, one on one, with about a dozen people at any one time, sharing my experiences of becoming sober. I would talk only with those who approached me for help and would try never to talk down to anyone, even if he was still using drugs or drinking. I believed if they wanted to discuss their problem, then they must have had a desire to quit, so I just tried to answer their questions. They could not believe that anyone could go without alcohol or drugs for sixteen years, as I have, and they become fascinated. Most were older men by prison standards, in their late twenties or thirties, and had been doing time in some correctional institution since they were children. I would see them watching me, waiting for a time when I was about to sneak a joint or drink some pruno. When it didn't happen, they would usually approach me cautiously, telling me they had a friend on the outside with a problem. The simple idea that they should stop shooting heroin and stop going to prison usually had never occurred to them. Others were desperately searching, but experience had taught them to trust no one. For some, though, I'm different; I'm an inmate too. One who had shown not only that he didn't drink or use, but that he could hold his mud-that is, keep his mouth shut.

I met every Saturday morning on the yard with each individual I worked with, and we discussed the Twelve Steps, usually the first half of the First Step:"Admitted we were powerless over addiction and obsession." Admitting they could be powerless over anything was a strange concept, even with the preponderance of evidence all around them. I would attempt to stress that they have spent the major portion of their adult lives in a prison or institution because of their addiction, that fact alone should convince anyone how powerless they had become over it. Saturday was convenient for me; as that was the morning I washed my clothes and hung them on the line to dry. Since it was necessary to keep your eye on the laundry to avoid having it stolen, I always spent a pleasant Saturday morning discussing the merits of being clean and sober while watching my clothes dry. So even if no one ever found sobriety, it wasn't a complete waste of time. The friend who shared my written inventory on the visiting yard returned periodically and served as my jailhouse spiritual advisor. We corresponded two or three times a week, but his visits were always pleasant, and I looked forward to them. We would go over the brief daily moral inventories I had continued to write. Each morning I would meditate beforehand for five minutes, then I would ask my God for the ability to live the coming day with inspiration and intuitive thoughts. At that time, I would review my actions and thoughts of the previous day, writing briefly about the areas in which I could improve my attitude and admitting to the continuing feelings of self-pity and anger that crept into my mind. Before I apologized or made amends to anyone I felt I might have harmed through my actions, I would discuss these matters with my friend, either through letters or his visits to find the exact nature, rather than evaluate the truth of my actions through my own jaded perspective. To do so required setting up a routine each morning, but I finally came to the point where I have been able to accomplish, at least in a small way, the suggestion in the Tenth Step:"Continued to take personal inventory and when wrong, promptly admitted it."

I've come to realize that to ever have the spiritual awakening to which the first line of the Twelfth Step refers—"Having had a spiritual awakening as a result of these steps…,"—I must integrate the Eleventh Step into my life and make it a working part of my mind: Sought through prayer and meditation to improve our conscious contact with God, as we understood Him, praying only for knowledge of His will for us and them power to carry that out?.

It was awesome to think that the only thing that I really should pray for is God?s will for me and the power to carry it out. It seems that I should be praying for someone or something; that is the way I have always understood prayer. It has suddenly dawned on me that true spiritual discipline is the ability to do nothing, asking God to guide me without question. The ultimate discipline is completely giving up control, even when I think it is for something good. I am slowly coming to the realization that after all is said and done, I have absolutely no conception of what truly transpires in this universe around me; that I am completely dependent on this God, whoever that may be, and accept that if I stop struggling to solve problems and difficulties, they will simply disappear.

I know that I will never even come close to that lofty place in life; the past few years have shown that, left to my own devices, I will always create chaos; even my best thinking gets me in trouble. I have prayed hard to become inspirational and intuitive, just trying to understand what my Higher Power's knowledge is for me. I am sure that at times I achieve that place; yet, as I read what I wrote sitting in the cell in Folsom and I examine my true motives, it is apparent that I was not completely honest. Being honest, especially with myself, is difficult and terribly elusive. Nevertheless, I am convinced that the searching for a conscious contact each day will bring me the peace I desire.

In that little room so many years ago, I was given the gift of sobriety. I am beginning to sense that, as precious as that gift is to me, I retained, over the years, the emotions of that ten-year-old boy running around the ghettos of San Francisco during the Depression-hanging around street corners, fighting, watching movies, dreaming of dancing in New York like Fred Astaire. Those emotions were probably just fine for a ten-year-old boy. But my emotional level did not change much with physical sobriety. When I was arrested at forty-eight-years-old, my emotional sobriety appeared to regress. Under the heavy stress of those arrests, I simply substituted, for my physical addiction, the obsession of Cops and Robbers.

The Eleventh Step has been the key to understanding the fulfillment of all the steps for me. That fulfillment comes from the continuing and active search for my God, knowing that I will discover only a minuscule portion of His will for me, yet realizing that the happiness comes from the seeking. This Step has begun to mold all the others together and bring me the spiritual discipline I need to live joyously in this world.

My daily five minute, 4:30 a.m. meditations, prayers, and writings not only have made my stay bearable, but also have turned the past two years of incarceration into one of my life's richest experiences. I'll never be the same person I remember so many years ago, just before the arrest: I am much closer to Ginger and the children than ever before; I know that whatever time it takes I will find a way to make the proper amends to my friend Fred; I no longer harbor resentments against my son-in-law, or anyone in the law enforcement or judicial systems. Today

I enjoy being with Maddog Costanzo, with all the swaggering and swearing, all the seeming defects of character, and all the love and compassion I know I hold in my heart. The Twelfth Step advises that "Having had a spiritual awakening as a result of these steps, we tried to carry this message to other (obsessive persons), and to practice these principles in all our affairs." I believe I truly have had a spiritual awakening as a result of doing these steps this time, and it came in the form of certain "Promises" I had read about in the same spiritual book that discusses inspiration and intuitive thought. They always will occur by working the Twelve Steps: We are going to know a new freedom and a new happiness. We will not regret the past nor wish to shut the door on it. We will comprehend the word serenity and we will know peace. No matter how far down the scale we have gone, we will see how our experience can benefit others. That feeling of uselessness and self-pity will disappear. We will lose interest in selfish things and gain interest in our fellows. Self-seeking will slip away. Our whole outlook and attitude on life will change. Fear of people and economic insecurity will leave us. We will intuitively know how to handle situations which used to baffle us. We will suddenly realize that God is doing for us what we could not do for ourselves. I don't believe that I have ever been as happy as I am at this moment. I am convinced that doing the Twelve Steps, even under the conditions that I have experienced over the last few years, is the reason the promises have been fulfilled for me in a most unlikely place-prison! I believe my emotional sobriety is progressing.

I will be released in the morning to the waiting arms of Ginger and my family. I hope to devote my life to working with individuals in the throes of addiction and obsession, sharing my experience, strength, and hope. Trying to help them understand that there is no situation so bad that it cannot be overcome by finding a personal Higher Power, through the spiritual discipline of the Twelve Steps.

Finally, I plan to continue to ask my God to help me practice in all my affairs the principles I have learned-although I must admit that I have been unable to thoroughly define them yet-asking only for His will for me and the power to carry it out; so that in the future I will know to take shelter, even though the day seems to be sunny and bright, when I hear the rustling of leaves.

# *Epilogue*

Petaluma, California, February, 1991, There are at least two groups of people I trust to do exactly the same thing on every occasion, under the same set of circumstances: junkies and new convicts. The addict is completely trustworthy. If you give him twenty dollars, he will immediately buy dope. The other group-the new generation of convicts, of which I am one-will always, when asked, unequivocally deny that they are guilty of crimes serious enough to get them into such an awful predicament. Older convicts, by contrast, usually take some pride in their craft and will answer that they are hit men, thieves, or bunco artists, whatever applies.

When I first began to think about recounting my adventures in dealing with law enforcement, I was advised either to confess my guilt or declare my innocence right from the beginning. Fat chance. I am one of those new convicts. I wanted the reader to know, in no uncertain terms, that my incarceration should be blamed on forces beyond my control: if only my attorney had done something different; law enforcement was out to get me; all the evidence was circumstantial; I came from a poor family and didn't know right from wrong; I even considered using the excuse that my high school social studies teacher didn't understand me. Anything that would relieve me of my own responsibility in the adventure.

Because of my enormous ego, I know it would be hard to admit guilt in anything I do. It is especially difficult when throughout the whole judicial process I held on to the idea that I was innocent. It would seem simpler and easier to just admit guilt and be done with it. After all, I have already been convicted, and have done the time. I doubt anyone would believe I'm innocent, anyway. Still, I am unable to make the admission. There would seem to be only two reasons to hesitate: either my ego will not let me, or I am, in fact, not guilty. I have attempted to depict my personality as it is-a highly addictive, obsessive, and emotional person. Since the case against me was based on circumstantial evidence that tried to show my state of mind when the alleged crimes were committed, I leave it up to the readers to create their own personal version of my state of mind before I attempted to rework the Twelve Steps.

Keeping firmly in mind that I am one of those new generation of convicts who will always deny involvement in the crime in which they have been accused, I personally believe that I was innocent of any criminal wrong in this case.

Over the three years after being released from prison, I can look back on my life and realize that I have been guilty of crimes as bad or worse than what I had been accused and convicted. I'm grateful now to be able to pay in later years for some of the things I did when I was younger. Had I been arrested and convicted then, my young family would have had to face life without me. Now that the children are all grown, the burden of my incarceration to my family was infinitely lessened. Not a day passes that I do not thank God for such a blessing.

The prosecutors who handled the case against me did a poor job of investigation, but they were successful in spite of themselves. I have always lived a high-profile life. In business I have been loud and obnoxious and made enemies. It would have been a simple task to find a reason to arrest me, dig through the records for information to support any theory the authorities wished to pursue, and find enough witnesses to testify. Eventually, that is what they were forced to do anyway. But in the beginning they were lazy and prosecuted me by intimidating, arresting, or threatening to arrest innocent people, and in effect holding them for ransom. I do not question the right, or even the duty, of the prosecutors to arrest me; I can't even say that I'm terribly unhappy about the outcome. But I was the only one who required prosecution, and law enforcement was aware of that fact, despite their harassment of Ginger, Fred, and my daughter.

Fred still practices law in San Francisco, but he has seen fit to end our former close friendship. While in my total Godless and distraught mental state at Chino, just after learning that the document was missing from the County Clerk's office, and that I would not be released on an appeal bond, I wrote him a nasty letter which I regretted almost as soon as it was sent. He is still my friend, I know that, and I don't require a physical relationship to validate that friendship. My daughter Caren and her husband have divorced. She has become a very successful executive and mother. Her former husband, Larry, continues to practice law. I have not seen him since my release, but I certainly wish him the best.

I have not inquired, yet, as to how the Kid, the Fox, or any of the judges are faring. I have the feeling that they all continue to play Cops and Robbers. I assume it is my fear of being dragged back into the game that prevents me from calling John for the information about them. It is strange that even though over three years have passed since my release, that fear continues to plague me. Oh well, I guess healthy fear is not an unreasonable emotion. Still, I know some day soon it will become necessary to make my amends to them. One thing that has taken place is that I have been able to define my own personal principles in a rudimentary sort of way. I'm sure I will add to the list from time to time as I understand myself better. In the meantime the following seem to work pretty well: Truth: My First Step was based on the truth. Not the truth my mind told me, and certainly not the truth that included right, wrong, good, and bad; defined by my own emotion and life experiences. I realize more and more that truth is the language of my God. I receive this truth through prayer, meditation, and daily personal writing; I hear it when my God speaks to me through others; it is revealed to me through a spiritual experience; it is apparent to me when, even though the world is telling me I am wrong, I have a warm glow inside my being that assures me that things are the way they should be. Truth was the first basic principle the Twelve Steps taught me.

Hope. Hope is what I receive when, after prayer and meditation, I write a list of the wonderments in my life. Trying to comprehend that God, as I understand Him, made a perfect world, and I am on a never ending search for that perfection. Experiencing the happiness and peace that always exist for me if I believe. All things that happen are gifts from that God, and if I'm able to put myself into the proper spiritual mood I will be able to recognize them as such.

Faith. While sitting in church with my grandchildren a few months ago, the pastor attempted to demonstrate faith. He asked a little girl in a little fluffy dress to come up in front of the church and stand on a chair. He then asked her, "Do you believe that if you fell off the chair, God and I will catch you?"

The little girl never hesitated and replied, "Oh yes, Father."

The pastor immediately said to her, "Then fall."

The girl became very flush, not knowing what to do, looking out into the congregation for her parents to tell her, but the churchgoers remained very still as they watched her reaction, anticipating her next move.

All of a sudden she just fell forward and the pastor caught her, turned to everyone with the girl in his arms and said, "And that is all faith is."

My personal goal is to have the faith of that child and fall when asked-even though the inadequate faith I have today convinces me that the pastor would never have had the strength to catch me.

Compassion/Service: I will never close the door to the events that took place in that little room, or most of the madness that proceeded them. They are the truth of my life, and I think of them without regret. Those events remind me of the suffering and pain that addiction and obsession continue to create in the lives of others. I realize that by simply sharing what happened to me, and how I recovered, I might be able to help relieve someone else's suffering and pain.

I have listened to people say that they share their experience, strength, and hope with another to keep themselves free of addiction and obsession, even if they are unable to help the person they are talking with. That is not one of my personal beliefs, much less one of my principles. I try to give help with total compassion for the person I'm talking with, without expectation, and without regard to what gain I might receive. Unless my assistance is unconditional, I have nothing to give, therefore, will never receive anything for myself. If I maintain unconditional compassion for another's pain, I have faith that my personal God will know what is right for me, and will deal with my sobriety in His own way. That is His business, not mine.

Honesty. I try to be as honest as I am able, but when I listed honesty as a principle I became uncomfortable. I meditated, then wrote about the uncomfortable feeling in my journal for several days. In addition, a great debate raged inside my head. "Honesty has to be listed as a principle, right?" I said to myself. "Wrong," said that intuitive voice. "But you don't understand," I replied to the voice. "Oh yes I do," the voice answered. "Keep meditating and writing about it." Becoming exasperated, I said, "But I've written all I can, and I'm still at a dead end."

Suddenly, my sweet little inspirational voice bellowed, "Then call your sponsor, discuss it with him, and your Higher Power to find the exact nature of your problem, you jerk." "Oh, that's probably a good idea. Why didn't I think of that?" I answered meekly. (Conversations like that happen all the time in my head.)

After the discussion with my sponsor I realized some very vital information about my personal principles. Honesty, over which I have some personal say, is a virtue in my life. Truth, which I receive directly from God is a principle. I can repeat something that I believe to be true, but is not, and still be perfectly honest. I will never be able to say something that isn't true, and still be truthful. My intuitive voice won again.

Humility. This very day I am celebrating the twentieth anniversary of finding my personal sobriety in that crummy little room. Today I also have come to the place on the list where I am writing about the principle of humility: the one principle I attempt to practice in all my affairs, but always fall short. Since I do not believe in coincidences, but believe all things happen for a purpose, I think I had better not put this writing off until tomorrow when I will be less emotional. I think that my inspirational voice is telling me to forge ahead now, saying just what comes to my mind, and live with the results. I am sitting here this morning, with tears in my eyes, unable to explain what the Twelve Steps have meant to me. That is something that I have experienced, and will never adequately put into words. They have served-and will continue to serve-as a beacon down a pathway leading to God. At times, during those years, the beacon has dimmed, but I would eventually discover that it was me, not God, whose eyes had closed. I would be frightened, still, I would force myself to open my eyes; only to see the beacon burning brightly as ever, showing me the way to a happiness such as I feel this morning. I would like to always acknowledge the cloak of love my God has wrapped around me whenever I felt frightened and alone. Although I know from sad experience that I am unable to even acknowledge a minute part of that love. Even so, right now-right this very instant-I feel happier than I have ever been in my whole life. I know that it is due to the love my God feels for me. I haven't enough gratitude to fully thank the thousands of people who have helped me along the way-from the man and woman who first found me in that little room, to the newcomer I met yesterday who I helped flush all his mind-altering pills down the toilet, determined to find a better life through the Twelve Steps-much less express the gratitude I feel for my God who was ultimately responsible. There is one person that I must mention, though, and that is my wife, Ginger, who obviously is celebrating her own twentieth anniversary in her own twelve step program. To paraphrase one of the greatest speakers I have ever heard-she came into the cave where I was hiding to find me, and held my hand in the dark, until we walked out together into the light of God.

It is quite apparent upon reading this list that the final principle would have to be love; unconditional love, without expectation. I see glimpses of it on occasion and am sure that the closer I am able to grasp such a concept, the closer I become an instrument of my God's will.

www.ingramcontent.com/pod-product-compliance
Lightning Source LLC
Chambersburg PA
CBHW020912290526
45784CB00002BA/517